Community Development Arenas in Singapore

Other Related Titles from World Scientific

Critical Issues in Asset Building in Singapore's Development
edited by S Vasoo and Bilveer Singh
ISBN: 978-981-3239-75-3

Collected Readings on Community Development in Singapore
edited by S Vasoo
ISBN: 978-981-120-382-4
ISBN: 978-981-120-459-3 (pbk)

How Working Together Matters: Adversity, Aspiration, Action
edited by David Chan
foreword by Lee Hsien Loong
ISBN: 978-981-3278-40-0

50 Years of Social Issues in Singapore
edited by David Chan
foreword by Tharman Shanmugaratnam
ISBN: 978-981-4696-91-3 (box-set)
ISBN: 978-981-4632-60-7
ISBN: 978-981-4632-61-4 (pbk)

Social Futures of Singapore Society
edited by David Chan
ISBN: 978-981-3222-22-9

Community Development Arenas in Singapore

S Vasoo
Bilveer Singh
Chan Xian Jie

World Scientific

NEW JERSEY · LONDON · SINGAPORE · BEIJING · SHANGHAI · HONG KONG · TAIPEI · CHENNAI · TOKYO

Published by

World Scientific Publishing Co. Pte. Ltd.

5 Toh Tuck Link, Singapore 596224

USA office: 27 Warren Street, Suite 401-402, Hackensack, NJ 07601

UK office: 57 Shelton Street, Covent Garden, London WC2H 9HE

Library of Congress Cataloging-in-Publication Data
Names: Vasoo, S., editor. | Singh, Bilveer, 1956– editor. | Chan, Xian Jie, editor.
Title: Community development arenas in Singapore / S Vasoo, Bilveer Singh, Chan Xian Jie.
Description: New Jersey : World Scientific, [2019] | Includes bibliographical references.
Identifiers: LCCN 2019024348 | ISBN 9789811204111 (hardcover) | ISBN 9789811204128 (ebook)
Subjects: LCSH: Community development--Singapore.
Classification: LCC HN700.67.Z9 C683 2019 | DDC 307.1/4095957--dc23
LC record available at https://lccn.loc.gov/2019024348

British Library Cataloguing-in-Publication Data
A catalogue record for this book is available from the British Library.

Copyright © 2019 by World Scientific Publishing Co. Pte. Ltd.

All rights reserved. This book, or parts thereof, may not be reproduced in any form or by any means, electronic or mechanical, including photocopying, recording or any information storage and retrieval system now known or to be invented, without written permission from the publisher.

For photocopying of material in this volume, please pay a copying fee through the Copyright Clearance Center, Inc., 222 Rosewood Drive, Danvers, MA 01923, USA. In this case permission to photocopy is not required from the publisher.

For any available supplementary material, please visit
https://www.worldscientific.com/worldscibooks/10.1142/11379#t=suppl

Desk Editor: Jiang Yulin

Typeset by Stallion Press
Email: enquiries@stallionpress.com

Printed in Singapore

About the Editors

S Vasoo is Associate Professorial Fellow at the Department of Social Work, National University of Singapore. He obtained his Doctorate and Master of Social Work from the University of Hong Kong and holds a Diploma in Social Studies with distinction from the University of Singapore. He authored a number of monographs on social issues and has published various such articles both internationally and locally. He was awarded the Honorary Life Member of the Singapore Association of Social Workers for his outstanding contributions to social work in Singapore. He was the Member of Parliament from 1984 to 2001 and he also served as Chairman of Government Parliamentary Committee for Community Development. He is Advisor to a number of Voluntary Welfare Organisations in Singapore and still actively involved in community development work and activities.

Bilveer Singh is a Singapore citizen, an Associate Professor at the Department of Political Science, National University of Singapore. He is concurrently an Adjunct Senior Fellow at the Centre of Excellence for National Security, S. Rajaratnam School of International Studies, Nanyang Technological University and the President, Political Science Association, Singapore. He received his MA and PhD in International Relations from the Australian National University. He has been lecturing on issues relating to Singapore's politics and foreign policy for more than 35 years.

He researches and publishes on Comparative Politics and International Relations and some of his works include: *Understanding Singapore Politics*, Singapore: World Scientific, 2017; *Quest for Political Power: Communist Subversion and Militancy in Singapore*, Singapore: Marshall Cavendish, 2015; *Politics and Governance in Singapore: An Introduction*, Second Edition, Singapore: McGraw-Hill Education Asia, 2012; *Politics and Governance in Singapore: An Introduction*, Singapore: McGraw-Hill Education, 2007.

Chan Xian Jie is a practicing social worker working in TRANS Family Services and also an Adjunct Lecturer in the Department of Social Work, National Universitay of Singapore. He lectures on community work practice and actively employs community organising ideas in his work to collaborate with citizens for collective action. He graduated from the University of Pennsylvania with a Master of Social Work and Master of Science in Social Policy in 2016. Since graduating with a Bachelor of Social Science (Hons.) in Social Work from the National University of Singapore in 2011, Xian Jie has developed an avid interest in the issue of homelessness during his practice experiences in the family service centre sector. His practice interests include the use of community organising approaches, applying critical theories to understand social issues, and conducting practice research.

About the Contributors

Belinda Choh Hiang Tan has over 15 years of social service experiences in the eldercare, children, youth, family and caregiver sectors. Her experiences range from service planning, implementation, fund-raising as well as corporate communications in the National Council of Social Service. She was also instrumental in the development of the Social Service Training Institute into a Continuing Education and Training (CET) centre. Today, she is responsible for the fund allocation of over $350 million government and community funds to support social services. During her stint in Montfort Care, Belinda was responsible for the YAH! (Young-At-Heart) and GoodLife! Makan eldercare service planning and operations. Belinda has a Master of Health Science, Gerontology, from the University of Sydney and BA degree from the National University of Singapore.

Elisha Paul Teo is a registered senior social worker at AMKFSC Community Services Ltd. He has a Master in Narrative Therapy and Community Work from the University of Melbourne. Paul is passionate in incorporating narrative and assets-based community development approaches with individuals, communities and stakeholders. He leads a team of social work practitioners and partners in working with community residents to find creative ways of reaching out to their neighbours. Paul and his community residents are invited from time to time to share about their community work with social work undergraduates at the National

University of Singapore and the social work master/post graduates from the Singapore University of Social Sciences.

Eugene Shum is Chief Community Development Officer at Changi General Hospital and Director, Community Partnership at SingHealth Office of Regional Health. He is a public health physician and Adjunct Associate Professor at the Saw Swee Hock School of Public Health, National University of Singapore. Dr Shum led the development of the Neighbours for Active Living Programme, an innovative health and social integration programme that supports residents with high care needs in the community. Dr Shum also led the development of Care Line, a 24/7 urgent assist-telecare service to keep seniors safe and provide them with peace of mind.

Francesca Phoebe Wah is a passionate individual with a caring heart for the community. A teacher by profession, but a trained social worker by conviction, Francesca founded Bringing Love to Every Single Soul (BLESS), a non-profit organisation that actively engages the community with an aim to engage, enrich and empower the lives of the less privileged. She graduated with a Masters in Social Work, specialising in family and community development.

Goh Soon Noi, Head of the Medical Social Services in Changi General Hospital has worked nearly 40 years in various settings including voluntary welfare organisations, restructured hospitals and in acute, sub-acute/rehabilitation and mental health outfits. Her work spans direct clinical practice, developing new services, supervising and mentoring social workers, education, research, planning and administration. Soon Noi also holds appointments in committees at SingHealth cluster level, in the social work professional body, voluntary welfare organisations and in Ministry of Health and Ministry of Social and Family Development.

Helen Keng Ling Sim is a Research Associate with Social Service Research Centre and Assistant Director of Fei Yue Family Service Centre. She has more than 18 years of experience in the social service sector, and was Head (Research) with the National Youth Council. She has served as volunteer consultant for social service agencies interested in developing their research capabilities. Her current research interests include youth and elderly participation as well as issues related to social work practice.

Irene Y. H. Ng is an Associate Professor of Social Work and Director of the Social Service Research Centre in the National University of Singapore. She holds a joint Ph.D. in Social Work and Economics from the University of Michigan. Her research areas include poverty and inequality, intergenerational mobility, and social welfare policy. Her research projects include an evaluation of a national Work Support programme; National Youth Surveys 2010, 2013 and 2016; a study of low-income households with debt; and an evaluation of Social Service Offices. She is active in the community, serving or having served in committees in the Ministry of Social and Family Development, National Council of Social Service, Ministry of Manpower, and various voluntary welfare organisations.

Mohamed Fareez is presently a Senior Assistant Director with AMKFSC Community Services Ltd. He obtained his Masters in Social Work (National University of Singapore) and a Master in Narrative Therapy and Community Work (University of Melbourne). Fareez is also an international faculty member of Dulwich Centre based in Adelaide, Australia and a certified Gallup StrengthsFinder coach. Fareez received the Promising Social Worker Award in 2011, and the Prime Minister Social Service Scholarship in 2012. Fareez was also awarded the outstanding newcomer award by the Community Mediation Centre in 2012.

Pravin Prakash is an Associate Research Fellow with the Centre of Excellence for National Security (CENS) at the S. Rajaratnam School of International Studies (RSIS), Singapore. He received his Master of Social Sciences in Political Science (with distinction) and his Bachelor of Social Sciences (with honours) in Political Science from the National University of Singapore (NUS). Pravin researches on issues relating to meritocracy, multiculturalism, identity politics, secularism, immigration, communal relations, ethno-religious nationalism and civil society in Singapore. He was a Teaching Assistant at the Department of Political Science, National University of Singapore, before joining RSIS.

Samuel Beng Teck Ng is the Founder/Chief Executive Officer of Montfort Care. His strength is in pioneering innovative social service programmes. In 2005, he established the first-ever learning college for the seniors — YAH! (Young-At-Heart) Community College. In 2016, he created a community kitchen for the stay-alone seniors, GoodLife! Makan. In 2018, he introduced a Mobile Home Bathing service for the immobile chronic sick elderly. In 2019, a Grief and Bereavement Centre was set up to champion end-of-life issues. In 2000, he was presented the Outstanding Social Worker Award. He was also conferred the Public Service Medal Award (PBM) and the Public Service Star (BBM) by the President of Singapore.

Sheean Chia graduated with a Bachelor of Social Sciences (Honours) in Social Work from the National University of Singapore. Sheean is currently a social worker at AMKFSC Community Services Ltd. Her main job scope includes casework and counselling as well as leading the Bakery Hearts Programme. Through her experience working with the women from Bakery Hearts, Sheean gains inspiration from stories filled in facing challenges, gaining strength and hope. Sheean looks forward to share her journey with Bakery Hearts and how it can continue to empower women in this programme.

Umardani bin Umle had worked in the offender rehabilitation sector for 10 years and he started out as a prison counsellor before he discovered his passion in community development work. He had been involved in several initiatives to enhance community rehabilitation of offenders and assist to uplift community agencies' capabilities to support the reintegration journey. He is currently a doctoral candidate in the field of Criminology, from the University of Glasgow. His research interest revolves around unpacking the decision-making process of social workers in the criminal justice system.

Zahara Mahmood, Principal Social Worker in Singapore Muslim Women Association Family Service Centre, has been in practice for the past 27 years. She has been actively advocating for women's rights and healthcare needs for the poor and needy. She has developed and run multiple initiatives to help marginalised individuals, including the children and youths from vulnerable backgrounds. She enjoys spending time with her social work colleagues in the field discussing cases, running support groups for families and volunteering in voluntary welfare organisations.

Contents

About the Editors v

About the Contributors vii

Introduction xv

Chapter 1	Some Challenges in Managing Volunteers and Enhancing Their Participation in the Social Service Sector in Singapore *S Vasoo*	1
Chapter 2	The Rise of a Political Community in Singapore *Bilveer Singh and Pravin Prakash*	19
Chapter 3	Mobilising Volunteers in Community Development *Francesca Phoebe Wah*	35
Chapter 4	Neighbours Programme: A Community Work Approach to Integrate Health and Social Services for Acute Care Hospital Patients *Goh Soon Noi, Zahara Mahmood and Eugene Shum*	51
Chapter 5	Developing the Social Capital of Young Drug Offenders: The PST (4Ks) Model *Umardani bin Umle*	69

Chapter 6	Using Narrative Practices in Community Development for Children and Families Living in Vulnerable Estates *Mohamed Fareez and Elisha Paul Teo*	85
Chapter 7	Community Development with Lifelong Learners in Action for Change *Samuel Beng Teck Ng and Belinda Choh Hiang Tan*	103
Chapter 8	Youth Participation in Community Development: Challenges and Potential *Helen Keng Ling Sim and Irene Y. H. Ng*	125
Chapter 9	Bakery Hearts: Lessons in the Intersections of Community Work and Social Entrepreneurship *Elisha Paul Teo and Sheean Chia*	145
Chapter 10	From "Homeless" to Survivalist: A Journey in Community Organising *Chan Xian Jie*	161
Chapter 11	The Future of Community Development: Issues and Challenges *S Vasoo*	179

Introduction

S Vasoo

In the last two decades, community development efforts in Singapore have been much focused on task-centred community activities, which mainly cover short-term projects revolving around socio-educational and recreational activities. Consequently, community organisations and groups have gravitated to become task- or programme-centred. Such an emphasis is further reinforced by the outsourcing of community services to the private sector, which has been contracted to deliver services or activities. The consequences, although not seen immediately, will be that in the longer term, it may reinforce learned helplessness of the participants or beneficiaries who are usually relegated to passive or dependent roles.

It must be noted that all communities have resources, which can be tapped. However, many community development efforts have not focussed on how these community resources, such as professional expertise in accountancy, finance and engineering, educational abilities, healthcare expertise, information technology capabilities, voluntary manpower, pools of retirees with varied experiences, green and horticultural expertise, communication personnel and human resources and financial managers, could be harnessed for the betterment of the community. The neglect in tapping these available community resources for doing community good will in the longer term create dependency on purchased services, which may not be affordable to some sectors of the community. In promoting active community development efforts to mobilise as many community resources as available, we will be able to strengthen the mutual help and support for one another and hence improve the social health of our community in different urban settings. Community development has to be progressive in taking both remedial and preventive steps in community problem solving and development, rather than being reactive in its approach where social and community workers undertake a fire-fighting strategy only when a fire has occurred, that is, dealing with the symptoms of the community's problem and not with the cause.

Singapore's demography is ageing dramatically and we are likely to have three out of 10 people to be above 65 years old. Use of technology to help the seniors to work and to live independently as long as possible in the community must be encouraged and supported. Various community groups can be supported to find feasible user-friendly technology to help the seniors to be more mobile and provide helpful aides to their activities of daily living. Community grants can be allocated to community groups that are looking into ways to produce innovative solutions to assist the seniors to work and live in place. Besides just technological innovations to support seniors to continue living independently, we must not ignore that there are many seniors who have varied expertise and resources, which can be tapped for promoting community activities. Seniors form a valuable pool of human talent that could be sourced by the community and social organisations for philanthropic and civic activities. Somehow, many community organisations tend to see seniors as a liability and not as a resource that can contribute to both personal and community well-being. As a result, the involvement of seniors is rather dismal and not encouraging, even though a large number of them are willing to volunteer. More often, the seniors are made to be passive recipients of services and not active givers of services.

Community development efforts could also be directed towards the promotion of more community cooperatives. Such cooperatives can be developed by interested residents in a number of areas such as childcare, home care, recycling, educational enrichment, home help, maintenance and repairs, home baking, laundry services and home-delivery services.

The growth of such community-based cooperatives is not encouraging and Community Development Councils (CDCs) can provide start-up grants for their establishment in our housing neighbourhoods. One may say there are social enterprises being encouraged but they are less cost-beneficial to consumers, as they are largely profit-driven. Cooperatives will be run by residents and would be membership-based for a collective purpose in the interest of residents.

We also observe that there is a rising social inequality, and the community development efforts can help here in some ways to mitigate against the gaps widening. Community development efforts can contribute to enlisting those who have and are capable to be involved to contribute their surplus resources, either in terms of funds or expertise to uplift those who need support to improve their social situation. Those who have can contribute to the community development fund or community betterment activities that can bring about change to the lives of those less well off. In this way, we can help to reduce the social gap through mutual community care and support. In short, we can help to promote a caring society.

In anticipation that our Singapore society will become more digital and with the emergence of disruptive economies, there is an urgency for community development efforts and practice to pay more attention to the use of aggregative technologies, to carry out social analytics to appreciate the impact of the changing needs and demographic profiles on the demands and delivery of social and community services. Through aggregative technology, we will be able to set up a Social Exchange Bank (SEB) wherein people can offer services and expertise to those who need services and expertise to help meet social needs. Through such a SEB managed via artificial intelligence, we can efficiently respond to those who need social services. An affordable fee could be charged for the services rendered to meet a social need. The setting up of the SEB is cost-effective, and it can be a new social exchange vehicle to reach out efficiently and cost-effectively to the people in need of services in the community.

In order that community participation in philanthropic activities or in volunteering in community development efforts can be taken to a higher level and greater institutional visibility, more resources and steps must be accorded to community organisations to drive this social engine. The challenge will be to redirect our community development approach to one which is more community- or resident-centric in our community work intervention. In short, more reaching-out to people or community groups should be undertaken. Therefore, this publication of collected essays on community development efforts in various arenas such as health, housing, community integration and bonding, building social support networks, ageing, crime and delinquency, social inclusions and social enterprises, will open up a wider horizon for community development efforts, than hanging on to the tail-end of social events or sticking to a remedial end of things. Discussions by various human service professionals and community social workers on the different challenges faced in promoting community development intervention in the aforementioned arenas will provide a reservoir of ideas and strategies to build a stronger and resilient community, which is more effective in problem solving.

The publication is structured, not based on any particular focus, but aimed at bringing out the importance and approach to community development in Singapore. The study begins with a review of the key issues and challenges in community development in Singapore by S. Vasoo. This is followed by a discussion of political community building by Bilveer Singh and Pravin Prakash. In Chapter 3, Francesca Phoebe Wah discusses the challenges of mobilising volunteers in community development. This is followed by a discussion of the neighbours' approach to integrating health and social services for acute care hospital patients by Goh Soon Noi, Zahara Mahmood and Eugene Shum. Chapter 5 discusses the management of young drug offenders by Umardani bin Umle, through an approach called the Parent Support Talk (PST). This is followed by a discussion by Mohamed Fareez and Elisha Paul Teo on the use of narratives in community development for children and families living in vulnerable estates. In Chapter 7, Samuel Beng Teck Ng and Belinda Choh Hiang Tan discuss the role of lifelong learning in community development. In Chapter 8, Helen Keng Ling Sim and Irene Y. H. Ng analyse the role of youth participation in community development. This is followed by a discussion of the "Bakery Hearts" project by Elisha Paul Teo and

Sheean Chia as an examination of social entrepreneurship and community development. In Chapter 10, Chan Xian Jie discusses the issue of "homelessness" from a perspective of community development. Finally, in the conclusion, S Vasoo analyses the future of community development in terms of the key issues and challenges facing Singapore.

Chapter 1

Some Challenges in Managing Volunteers and Enhancing Their Participation in the Social Service Sector in Singapore

S Vasoo

Introduction

Many social and voluntary welfare organisations (VWOs) still take a lacklustre approach in managing and promoting the participation of volunteers who are more often than not seen as an organisational appendage, being viewed as a burden to the staff and a spent force which does not generate but consume more organisational resources.[1] Such a myopic viewpoint cannot go unchallenged as efforts of professional manpower can be more effective when complemented by volunteers who bring the human dimension in the delivery of social services. In all human miseries

---

[1] Volunteer participation is defined as efforts either on their own or jointly with those of government, corporate sector, community organisations, not-for-profit groups and/or VWOs to promote community betterment and community problem solving by involving people based on mutual help or self-help and planned changes. The outcome is community ownership in promoting community well-being.

and needs, both professionals and volunteers are required to find the most meaningful and cost-effective way in human development and problem solving. It is becoming noticeable that many agencies in the social and welfare sectors are outsourcing their services to service contractors and this can retard volunteerism, especially when we need to tamper communities to be less utilitarian and materialistic in extending social care and help for those in need.[2]

Volunteerism in social service sector efforts is focused much on task-centred community activities which mainly cover short-term projects involving socio-educational and recreational activities. Consequently, volunteer groups have gravitated to become task- or programme-centred. This is further reinforced by the outsourcing of community services to the private sector which has been contracted to deliver services or activities. The consequences of such an approach can reinforce learned helplessness of the beneficiaries who are usually relegated to passive or dependent roles.

Participation of volunteers has been undergoing significant transformation in the last few years as activities of clan and lineage organisations have declined despite recent efforts to encourage them to reform and rejuvenate.[3] In response to this situation, more formal voluntary social and welfare organisations have been and are being established to assist the disadvantaged sector of Singapore's community such as the disabled and sick, aged destitute, individuals and families in distress, and children and youth in need of care and guidance. Also, neighbourhood betterment activities undertaken by Residents' Committees (RCs) in the public

---

[2] Joyce Rothschild, Katherine K. Chen and David Horton Smith, "Avoiding bureaucratization and mission drift in associations", in David Horton Smith, Robert A. Stebbins and Jurgen Grotz (eds.), *The Palgrave Handbook of Volunteering, Civic Participation, and Non-Profit Associations* (New York: Palgrave Macmillan, 2016), pp. 1007–1024.

[3] Milton J. Esman, "Development administration and constituency organisation", *Public Administration Review*, 38(2), 1978, pp. 166–172; Seah Chee Meow, *Community Centres in Singapore: Their Political Involvement* (Singapore: Singapore University Press, 1973); S Vasoo, "Grassroots mobilization and citizen participation: Issues and challenges", *Community Development Journal*, 26(1), 1991, pp. 1–7.

housing estates have increased pointedly in the last decade.[4] The government's conscious policies in avoiding the welfarist model and emphasis on promoting self-help through the provision of tax exempt status, matching grant, land and capital cost, for selected voluntary social and welfare organisations, have contributed to the growth of voluntary efforts involving many helping hands to care for the unfortunate and less-abled citizens.

Addressing Volunteer Participation Issues

The observation that volunteerism participation in social services has become highly task-oriented, focussing on short-term projects, many of which are outsourced, has negatively affected volunteer participation in general. Such an orientation and drive is likely to dampen, if not reduce, volunteer commitment and motivation to help social service and welfare agencies to tackle prevailing community problems as well as emerging social issues and needs. In the long run, the spirit of community service and volunteerism will be eroded and each man will only care for himself and the axiom "all men are brothers", will end as no men will be brothers, and where each will only care for his own. This will lead to the rise of uncaring Singaporeans, making our society socially unhealthy.[5]

Consequences of Outsourcing Issue on Volunteerism

It is noted that there is an increasing trend by agencies to outsource community activities. Why is this the case? In the name of efficiency and

---

[4] R. Dan Sundblom, David Horton Smith, Per Selle, Christophe Dansac and Courtney Jensen, "Life cycles of individual associations", in David Horton Smith, Robert A. Stebbins and Jurgen Grotz (eds.), *The Palgrave Handbook of Volunteering, Civic Participation, and Non-Profit Associations* (New York: Palgrave Macmillan, 2016), pp. 950–974.

[5] Salma Akhter, Kunle Akingbola, Anna Domaradzka-Widla, Omar K. Kristmundsson, Chiku Malunga and Uzi Sasson, "Leadership and management of associations", in David Horton Smith, Robert A. Stebbins and Jurgen Grotz (eds.), *The Palgrave Handbook of Volunteering, Civic Participation, and Non-Profit Associations* (New York: Palgrave Macmillan, 2016), pp. 915–949.

the urgency for quick turn-over, agencies often face time constraints. Therefore, most community activities are planned within a short time frame and often tied to the term of office holders. Such an emphasis can make volunteer groups insular and not development-oriented. They then become task- or activity-centred, slowly digressing from being people-centred which is aimed at promoting self-help and community ownership of those who are beneficiaries of the community activities. As such, many social and voluntary organisations adopt a less outreaching approach to understand the changing needs of the community. In the longer term, such a move will make them more detached rather than keeping in touch with the needs of people or the client groups who are uninvolved or are vulnerable to social problems.[6]

Effects of Centralisation of Leadership and Population Ageing on Volunteerism

The leaders or those in management of social and voluntary sectors are generally left to a small group of elected office bearers to bear the responsibilities. Such a *de facto* style of management can lead to leadership centralisation. As such, the burdens of delivering community activities or not-for-profit projects are carried out by a small group of organisational leaders who will eventually be affected by compassion fatigue. More often than not, the leadership of the organisations in the social service sector does not rejuvenate and those in leadership stay entrenched for many terms as there are fewer younger members or others who are prepared to step into the leadership positions despite those in leadership positions wanting to give way. Somehow, the old leaders in the management circles continue and they then become the domineering force with the leadership becoming centralised in the hands of a few seniors who continue year in and year out to be retained to run the outfit in their old

---

[6] Howard J. Wiarda, Paul Adams, Lam Wai-Man and Dwight Wilson, "Corporatism versus pluralism and authoritarianism as association contexts", in David Horton Smith, Robert A. Stebbins and Jurgen Grotz (eds.), *The Palgrave Handbook of Volunteering, Civic Participation, and Non-Profit Associations* (New York: Palgrave Macmillan, 2016), pp. 1116–1138.

traditional or conservative style. To avert this situation, more attention should be devoted by the leadership to encourage and enlist more resourceful and interested people to head different service projects to deal with community needs and concerns. To help a smoother transition of leadership in the sector, it will be prudent to have guidelines to volunteer leaders in the organisation's board to implement an orderly change by inducting younger leaders on leading the organisation to deliver services which will meet new emerging social needs.

The issue of succession of leadership with fresh and younger leaders faced by many organisations in the social service sector will be addressed, provided appropriate steps are taken by incumbent boards which can sometimes be rather exclusive and protective of their turf. In the near future, the number of young volunteers will decline and this will affect the work of voluntary social and welfare organisations, which rely on younger volunteers for active programmes. This is because one of the most significant social phenomena facing Singapore in the immediate decade is population ageing. The population ageing trend is becoming conspicuous. In 1990, there were about 118,300 persons aged 60 years and above and by the turn of the year 2014, the number has increased to 431,601 persons.[7] It is estimated that there will be about 900,000 elderly, or about 25% of Singaporeans will be above the age of 60 years by 2030. The pool of younger adults available to be tapped for volunteers will drop dramatically because our population growth is declining due to lower fertility rate below replacement standing at about 1.5 persons. This serious drop below the replacement rate will create socio-economic consequences such as lack of manpower to produce goods and services and, more importantly, the availability of younger persons to provide care and support for the community of older people and families with seniors. The young will be so stretched in supporting the older family members that they will not be able to participate in voluntary services as they will have less discretionary time at their disposal than their counterparts in the preceding

---

[7] Department of Statistics, Population Trend 2014, Singapore, 2014; Yap Mui Teng and Christopher Gee, "Ageing in Singapore: Social issues and policy challenges", in David Chan (ed.), *50 Years of Social Issues in Singapore* (Singapore: World Scientific, 2015), pp. 3–10.

generation, who faced less time constraint and had more manpower to be enlisted as volunteers for altruistic activities. However, the reduction of young volunteers could be augmented by mobilising older persons who will form the potential pool for volunteer manpower. Currently, few organisations have a comprehensive plan in tapping the rich experience and expertise of our retired senior citizens. It is therefore desirable for our organisations to identify various voluntary activities for their involvement.[8]

Low Participation Rate and Demand for Volunteers' Limited Spare Time

It is observed that the rate of participation of volunteers, particularly young adults, is not significant and this could be due to the less tangible benefits to be gained directly by them from volunteering in community service programmes. The high participation of volunteers and beneficiaries is critical in ensuring the sustainability of community activities for community problem solving. Besides this issue, the social and voluntary sector must promote more concrete services to meet the beneficiaries' social and economic needs as this will address the public goods dilemma and reduce their cost of participation. When volunteer groups and organisations do not bear this in mind in their community service, both minorities and working class households will not be motivated to participate in some mainstream community projects such as literacy education, matched savings, environmental protection, provision of shelter, provision of sanitation, credit unions and cooperatives, potable and clean water, early childhood learning, infant and maternal healthcare, and preventive healthcare, vaccination, retirement planning, eldercare and vocational training.

However, with improvements in working conditions, Singaporeans are having more leisure time. At least 50% of the working Singaporeans have about 14 hours of leisure time per week. This can be tapped by various social and welfare organisations. In the light that leisure time is limited, Singaporeans are less likely to expend it in voluntary activities which

---

[8] R. Dan Sundblom, David Horton Smith, Per Selle, Christophe Dansac and Courtney Jensen, "Life cycles of individual associations", pp. 950–974.

are beneficial and useful.[9] It is therefore important for voluntary social and welfare organisations to make their voluntary service programmes interesting and an attractive and appealing experience for volunteers. Unless this is actively considered, they will not be able to attract and sustain volunteers. It has been found that organisations which offer mundane and routine voluntary service programmes cannot sustain the interest of volunteers longer than necessary.[10] The participation of volunteers in Singapore's voluntary social and welfare services is still rather low. It has been found that only 6% of the population between 15 and 55 years old are involved in voluntary work. This participation rate compares less favourably with other countries such as the United States of America, Japan and the United Kingdom, where the participation rates are 39%, 25% and 12%, respectively. The participation rate in all countries, including Singapore, will probably decline in the near future, and this will affect the work of voluntary social and welfare organisations which rely more on younger volunteers who face competing demands for their time. Robotic technology will surface to undertake work which is normally assigned to volunteers.

Implications of Lack of Coordination in Service Learning and Hollowing Out of Volunteerism Talents

Another significant issue that social service institutions have to address is the lack of concerted efforts to coordinate the many sprouting volunteer groups and voluntary organisations in providing community services. At the same time, these heart-string organisations have to compete with more lucrative and highly incentivised service exchange programmes, business and research projects. As a result, there is a hollowing out of the more resourceful and younger volunteer talents from the set-ups promoting philanthropic and community activities. In the recent years, many

---

[9] Mancur Olson, *The Logic of Collective Action: Public Goods and the Theory of Groups* (Massachusetts: Harvard University Press, 1965).
[10] Benjamin Gidron, "Sources of job satisfaction", *Journal of Voluntary Action*, 12(1), 1983, pp. 20–35; Goh Lee Gan, Kua Ee Heok, and Chiang Hai Ding, *Ageing in Singapore: The Next 50 Years* (Singapore: Spring Publishing Ltd., 2015).

businesses and large multinational corporations provide very attractive internship to employable young adults for work attachment and this siphons off many younger persons from tertiary institutions and social service sectors, which tend to offer less perks and incentives to engage them in service projects. These competing opportunities are becoming a reality. Therefore, the attraction of young volunteer talents away from the social service sector is unavoidable, but the challenge for the social service sector is to design more innovative projects to draw younger volunteer talents to participate in community problem solving and gain more intrinsic incentives for which monetary compensation does not measure up. A well coordinated and challenging resource bank for service and learning innovative projects, where both young and adult volunteers can get access and make a good informed choice and where they can be attached for a period of time to implement their prospective projects, is one way ahead. However, the older urban neighbourhoods are seeing a flowing out of the more capable who are resourceful, making the situation rather slackened with less able manpower to tackle the problems of the community. This being the situation, there will be limited good volunteer manpower to be mobilised for community problem solving.[11]

Effects of Inflexible Volunteering and Lack of Opportunities for Innovation

Over the years, it is observed that the social service sector, particularly many agencies, have grown and, in some cases, have become megaorganisations which have developed rules and regulations to manage staff and volunteers in delivering services to their consumers. Volunteer tasks become more rule-bound and the volunteering schedules are arranged for the convenience of paid personnel and not for tapping the volunteer manpower to meet the requirements of social service organisations. Therefore,

---

[11] Gabriel Berger, Leopoldo Blugerman, Guo Chao, Rumen Petrov and David Horton Smith, "Relationships and collaboration among associations", in David Horton Smith, Robert A. Stebbins and Jurgen Grotz (eds.), *The Palgrave Handbook of Volunteering, Civic Participation, and Non-Profit Associations* (New York: Palgrave Macmillan, 2016), pp. 1162–1187.

this straight-lace approach does not help to harness more volunteers who are responsive to flexible volunteering, and this is becoming more suitable to those volunteers whose talents can be enlisted for innovative projects. Increasingly, many professionals are involved in globalised jobs and their professional expertise in such areas as management, marketing, branding, fundraising, initiating sustainable social enterprises and data analytics can be garnered for philanthropic and voluntary activities. The social service sector will have to be less rigid in tapping a vast potential pool of volunteers who are skilled and capable of value-adding to the work of the sector which will ultimately lose out by remaining insular and unresponsive to the changing globalised work world. Also, more attempts must be made by the sector to encourage and enable professionals to have more opportunities to pilot community service projects which entail innovative ideas in services to meet needs of various disadvantaged and marginalised groups together with social and community workers. A wider and varied voluntary thoroughfare can help to accommodate diverse individual volunteers who will help the sector to become more effective in community problem solving.[12]

Some Steps on Enhancing Volunteer Management and Participation

In meeting some challenges confronting community development through enhancing the heart-string, a few ideas are proposed for key leaders in student volunteer groups and organisations to consider undertaking so as to enhance community development efforts in the various country settings.[13]

---

[12] David Horton Smith and Robert A. Stebbins, "Conclusions and future prospects", in David Horton Smith, Robert A. Stebbins and Jurgen Grotz (eds.), *The Palgrave Handbook of Volunteering, Civic Participation, and Non-Profit Associations* (New York: Palgrave Macmillan, 2016), pp. 1362–1390.

[13] David Horton Smith, Brent Never, Abu-Rumman Samir, Afaq K. Amer, Bethmann Steffen, Gavelin Karin, Heitman H. Jan, Jaishi Trishna, Ambalika D. Kutty, Jacob M. Paturyan, Rumen G. Petrov, Tereza Pospíšilová, Lars Svedberg and L. Torpe, "Scope and trends of volunteering and associations", in David Horton Smith, Robert A. Stebbins and Jurgen Grotz (eds.), *The Palgrave Handbook of Volunteering, Civic Participation, and Non-Profit Associations* (New York: Palgrave Macmillan, 2016), pp. 1241–1283.

Need for Setting-Up Volunteers' Management and Development Centre

Currently, there are community volunteer activities or service-learning activities that are not well-coordinated, and many activities are fractured and disjointed, leading to the involvement of students being rather punctuated. Recently, some tertiary educational institutions began paying more attention to service learning. But still inadequate resources are deployed to give credence to the importance of community service learning to imbue social responsibility in the young and promote corporate social responsibility (CSR) among institutions of higher learning. More serious efforts must be made to promote philanthropic passion in the young, and this will help our society to have more individuals who can lead and inspire others to be involved in community betterment and public good activities. To help drive and build philanthropic activities in tertiary educational institutions, a Centre for Philanthropic Activities can be established to recruit, train, promote and sustain philanthropic efforts. This will have to be a full-fledged centre run on a non-profit basis.

Enhancing Self-Help and Community Ownership

In carrying out community service activities, there should be fewer outsourcing contracts and more insourcing activities by mobilising students to form not-for-profit organisations or social enterprises. Such attempts will provide more opportunities for student volunteer groups and beneficiaries to participate in decision-making so that they all can take ownership. Community care groups and support networks can be formed. This will make beneficiaries not passive recipients of services and be engaged in problem solving. Student volunteer groups and organisations can widen the base of participation by beneficiaries helping to form various interest groups or task forces to work on various social issues and projects such as security watch and crime prevention, cooperative care services, improvements to recreational facilities, pollution control, thrift through microcredit groups and environmental enhancement projects. It will be useful where possible to encourage beneficiaries to take charge in finding more effective ways to deal with the local matters and with the support of the local councils. This will truly be promoting community development as local residents or beneficiaries will learn and find more realistic solutions to solve their specific needs and problems and become accountable for their decisions. However, with the move towards information technology (IT), people could become impersonal and more homebound, social interactions could be reduced and social bonding could be threatened. Therefore, all the more personalised outreaching efforts have to be complemented with online contacts.

Implications of Leadership Rejuvenation and Organisational Renewal to Volunteerism

It is also observed that a significant number of grassroots leaders of community organisations in the mature housing estates are above 50 years old. These organisations face difficulties in recruiting younger residents to take up leadership.[14] With the greying of the organisational leadership, there is urgency to rejuvenate the leadership of community organisations by attracting younger student talents to participate in them. It is not just sufficient to recruit them but they must be mentored by some committed older leaders. With attachment to specific mentors, student volunteers can be anchored to the organisations, and this will reduce attrition among those taking up leadership in organisations dominated by seniors. A rejuvenated leadership will continue to be vibrant and relevant to meet the needs and aspirations of the younger generation. We must also attract younger people-centred volunteers and potential leaders who can be given all the support to carry out community problem solving activities. People-centred volunteers and leaders are proactive and they should not be piled with so much tasks that they then suffer burnout. More importantly, volunteers should be given management skills training to understand the needs of beneficiaries so that they can help make community

---

[14] S Vasoo, *Neighbourhood Leaders Participation in Community Development* (Singapore: Academic Press, 1994).

organisations responsive to tackling emerging social needs.[15] It is crucial for each social and welfare organisation to set a Volunteer Management and Development Centre which will recruit, orientate, train, deploy, develop and recognise volunteers. Aggregation in IT can be put in place to match volunteers in terms of the services they offer with people in need of the service or help.

Volunteering to Reach-Out to Lower Income Residents and Minorities

As many countries are open economies and are becoming more globalised, it is inevitable that people with low skills are likely to face depressed wages, and this can lead to a widening income gap.[16] People with better skills are likely to move ahead, while those with low skills and those who are less literate in IT will fall behind in income. Social stratification based on social-economic classes confounded by ethnicity may surface if excessive free market competition is not tempered. As a consequence, social conflicts could emerge, and when this is capitalised by political and racial fanatics, our Singapore's community harmony and cohesion could be fractured.[17] As such, student groups and organisations, including community organisations, can take preventive measures to deliver community-based self-help programmes such as social and educational assistance, computer training, educational head start for children of low-income families, childcare services, youth vocational guidance and counselling programmes, family life and development activities and continuing learning programmes to help the socially disadvantaged groups. As a long-term Singapore measure for people-capability building, it is important for us to develop more educational head start projects for low-income children in the nursery age group. The increase of such

---

[15] Paul Colomy, Chen Huey-Tsyh and Gregg Andrews, "Situational facilities and volunteer work", *The Journal of Volunteer Administration*, 1987, pp. 20–25; Benjamin Gidron, "Sources of job satisfaction", pp. 20–35.

[16] Goh Chok Tong, *Prime Minister's National Day Rally Speech 2000* (Singapore Government: Ministry of Information and the Arts, 2000), pp. 22–25.

[17] Lee Kuan Yew, *From Third World to First: The Singapore Story, 1965–2000* (Singapore: Times Media, 2000), pp. 143–157.

projects through community partnership of various self-help groups, unions, cooperatives and not-for-profit organisations will help children from disadvantaged backgrounds to level up to acquire productive skills for their future livelihood. Matched savings schemes tied up with such projects can be initiated. These community development efforts can help reduce the social friction between classes and ethnic groups. Fanatics will find it less tempting to exploit the race card as the problems facing low-income families cut across all ethnic groups. So, the realistic solution is to help level up the capabilities of all disadvantaged children despite their colour or ethnicity.

Impact of Renewal and Rejuvenation of Ageing Neighbourhoods on Volunteering

It will be evident that in the next two decades, Singapore will see a number of silver neighbourhoods. If attempts by policymakers to renew and rejuvenate these neighbourhoods are slower than population ageing in these places, then these neighbourhoods will become listless and socially run-down. Local social and economic activities will slow down, and younger people will not be attracted to live in these neighbourhoods as seniors will dominate. Ultimately, there will be more families facing the need for care of elderly parents or relatives. As many of these families have working family members, they will face the burden of care. Social breakdowns are likely without accessible social support and community care services delivered at the local level. Therefore, there will be demands for more community-based programmes to cater to the needs of families who have frail-aged family members. The number of such families is expected to increase in the next decade. In light of this situation, student volunteer groups and organisations, and VWOs together with the involvement of residents as well as the hospitals, will have to work as partners to provide community care services such as home help, meals service, daycare, integrated housing and community nursing. Here, community care cooperatives could be formed to offer services which will be more convenient and accessible to the families with the frail elderly needing care and attention. There is potential for this type of social enterprise to be established with the participation of families as one of the stakeholders. Here, student groups with medical and other professional training have a role to play in the community's social and health betterment.

Volunteering in Early Intervention Educational and Parenting Programmes

Volunteers can play a significant role in early educational intervention and parenting programmes. Educational mentoring scheme of young children from working class and marginalised families can help them in a way to have some head start in life. Such efforts can help in some ways to mitigate the educational underachievement of children from poor and less literate families. As in Singapore society and elsewhere, there is a widening income gap and there is a population of new poor who are trapped in low wage contributed to an extent by imported cheap labour, low skills and educational level. These new poor have both family and social difficulties which unless addressed early can lead to various social consequences which will affect the social health of the community. Volunteers, both young and seniors, can be enlisted by Family Service Centres (FSCs) to collaborate with other community groups with the support of the Ministry of Education (MOE) and Ministry of Social and Family Development (MSF) to initiate early social and educational intervention programmes such as family mentoring, counselling, family life education, educational head start, care networks, income supplement projects and early reading. Through various educational enrichment by volunteers, more children in the low-income families can be targeted to benefit from early supportive education and literacy programmes. In the longer term, the social divide can be further widened when more of low-income children fail to acquire the knowledge and skills that can enable them to earn a competitive wage, thereby reducing the present Gini coefficient of 0.49 based on per-household member after discounting government transfers.[18] There is much potential for the various public housing estate neighbourhoods to encourage more able Singaporeans to support educational enrichment and early head start programmes to assist

---

[18] *Yearbook of Statistics Singapore*, 2017.

the young of the less able Singaporeans. Here, one can use Aggregated IT to cover the breadth and depth in meeting the most needy children who want a volunteer to mentor them. A good matching of those who have a need with those who can volunteer their service to meet such educational upliftment needs could be undertaken. In doing this, voluntary initiatives at a community-wide scale can prevent social fractures within our society and promote social transfers and bonding, demonstrating that there are volunteers who care.

Collective Fundraising Effort in Promoting Voluntary Effort

The establishment of centralised fundraising through Singapore Community Chest (SCC) was a good move to provide financial resources to the work of charities. This set-up does reduce duplication of volunteer drives to raise funds more efficiently but, in the process, has inadvertently affected the opportunities for involving more volunteers. Mega fundraising projects do not tap more volunteers than necessary to run the events as these are outsourced to event management companies. There is a place for centralised fundraising, but more organisations must have a share in the fundraising efforts and when they are decentralised, based on thematic funding appeals, more volunteer manpower could be cajoled to participate. In the long-run, volunteers across all societal levels have a part to play in the care and share in fundraising for a few major charitable causes each year. The place for volunteers in fundraising efforts must not be weaned-off from social and welfare organisations by too much emphasis on centralised fundraising as this will reinforce dependency on the SCC and volunteers' role in running many appeals for public funding support through various charities will wane. New emphases and opportunities for volunteer participation in fundraising for different social and charitable causes can be implemented through many charities and many volunteers of varied persuasions and social standings, the rich and not-so-rich, can play a part in fundraising activities. The view that too many fund charitable appeals can cause compassion fatigue does not hold but in fact can prod the social conscience of different sectors of society. Fundraising by volunteers and boards of management will also lead to greater public accountability of the utilisation of the funds raised from donations.

Conclusion: Future of Volunteerism

Volunteer participation and management are critical for the growth and development of the social service sectors including charities. Volunteer groups and organisations must also encourage beneficiaries to take ownership of the various social and economic activities which are delivered in the various neighbourhoods in partnership with a number of community groups. To have an impact, volunteer groups and organisations cannot continue to assume that they know what beneficiaries or residents want but should outreach to appraise their social needs or requirements. In short, community betterment and development should promote self-help, and the focus should be to encourage mutual help and not dependency and helplessness.

As various regions of the world have become more globalised, social needs and problems become more challenging to solve as it will require the efforts of a number of key players. Therefore, community problem solving will require the partnership of several parties and importantly a place for volunteers to play a role in community problem solving. The partnership model of the government, community organisations and volunteer groups and organisations, corporate sector and philanthropic individuals can be encouraged as such a model emphasises on the belief in sharing the social burdens. All partners involved in community problem solving have shared social responsibilities.

It will be anticipated that in older urban neighbourhoods there will be a demand for the care and support of the elderly who live on their own. There will be a lack of young voluntary manpower available for social and welfare agencies to rely on for carrying out helping activities, especially when the young will be burdened with work and caring for both their young children and elderly parents. Therefore, it will be prudent to build a reservoir of active seniors who can provide care and attention to the elderly requiring care and support. As for the emerging younger urban places, there will be younger persons and youth manpower resources, and hence, they can be approached to provide mutual help to ageing communities. This phenomenon will be the scenario in developing urban settings where the burden pertaining to the aged will be the issue to address, whereas in developing urban settings, there will be surplus younger manpower. So, a social exchange voluntary human service bank can be initiated.

A comprehensive outfit to recruit, deploy flexibly, recognise, train and develop volunteers for effective and meaningful voluntary social contributions will have a lasting impact for socially healthy communities in Singapore. In future, volunteer participation and management will be a click away and Aggregated IT will be used to effectively match volunteers based on their offer of services to those in need of help with appropriate service help. This aggregative systems technology will help enhance volunteer participation and management very efficiently and enable to deliver helping services to penetrate to persons in need of help. Hopefully, a personalised caring and helpful service could be given passionately with compassion.[19]

---

[19] David Horton Smith and Robert A. Stebbins, "Conclusions and future prospects", pp. 1362–1390.

Chapter 2

The Rise of a Political Community in Singapore

Bilveer Singh and Pravin Prakash

Introduction

The concept of political community is as old as mankind, even though how one defines it depends on the particular characteristics of its people, the stage of economic and social development it is in and hence, the critical importance of the context in which one is discussing the concept. In a way, the concept of political community, though important universally, also highlights the particularistic aspect in which a society finds itself in. Despite courting controversies and debates, Aristotle saw a political community as one "in which citizens take turns ruling and being ruled for the sake of living well, sharing together in the intrinsically valuable activity of participatory citizenship that is central to a fully flourishing human life".[1] For Aristotle, "participatory citizenship is an intrinsically valuable component of a good human life, and political community exists to foster it" and "justice demands that political participation be distributed to those who are best able to exercise it, and in many cases those best able to

---

[1] David J. Riesbeck, *Aristotle on Political Community* (London: Cambridge University Press, 2016).

exercise it are a small minority".[2] Aristotle defended kingship as an ideal form of government, something which in later days, critics saw as being inconsistent with his theory of justice. Still, Aristotle saw man, as a "thinking animal" and as a "political animal", living in a city (*polis*), a society that was governed by customs and laws. It was the quest to live in harmony that a "good life" would be achieved.

Drawing from the Aristotelian tradition, one can clearly argue for the importance of a political community. Aristotle also highlighted the importance of the political, economic and social domains as being the keys upon which a successful political community would be built up, even though from his perspective and partly due to his era, he saw kingship as an effective and best form of governance in a city-state. Fast-forwarding to the present era and in the context of one of the most successful city-states in the world today, it would be useful to overlay the concept of political community in Singapore and how it has emerged to this day. Basically, there are two key aspects that are worth noting, namely, the development or lack of development of a civil society and, second, how a political community has been constructed in a setting of chronic differences, fractures and pluralism to forge a political nation of a sort, something the political leaders continue to describe as being in a state of "work in progress".[3]

Civil Society in Singapore

The relationship between the citizen, civil society, politics and the Government in Singapore is a complicated one. This relationship has come under scrutiny in recent times, with much debate focusing on dynamics that exist between the political rights of the individual, the role of non-governmental organisations (NGOs) and civil society as well as the government's perspective.

---

[2] *Ibid.*
[3] Goh Chok Tong, "The Singapore nation: A work in progress", Speech at Marine Parade National Day Dinner, 19 August 2006 (Singapore: Singapore Government Media Release, 2006).

Conceptual Difficulties

The conceptual history of the term "civil society" is enmeshed with the idea of citizenship, the limits of state power and the regulation of market economies. The popular modern perspective is that civil society serves as a buffer zone between the state and market — a socio-political space strong enough to negotiate the influences of the government and the free market on the individual and greater society. Alexis de Tocqueville, in his landmark work, *Democracy in America* (1835) articulated the importance of what he referred to as *political society*, an indispensable third space that existed between the state and the modern capitalist economy, which allowed for the development of socio-political associations.[4] Tocqueville reflected on "the art of association" as the most important law that guides modern societies, providing the vital force and energy that sustain modern democratic societies by developing a strong sense of understanding and bonding within the body politic.[5] Critically, he noted that political society was essential in controlling the potential excesses of the state by functioning as the "independent eye of society" that watches over the public sphere.

Jurgen Habermas, the German sociologist and philosopher, articulated that "civil society is made up of more or less spontaneously created associations, organisations and movements, which find, take up, condense and amplify the resonance of social problems in private life, and pass it on to the political realm or public sphere".[6] An active civil society hence potentially functions as a bridge between the government and the people, encouraging positive discourse and initiatives.

Both Tocqueville and Habermas saw civil society as a critical space that allowed for the flourishing of an active citizenry, a vibrant social culture and a potential safeguard against the excesses of the modern state. Singapore's perspective on civil society, however, is undeniably Gramscian. Gramsci viewed civil society as an ideological space where consent,

---

[4] Alexis de Tocqueville and Arthur Goldhammer, *Democracy in America* (New York: Library of America, 2004).
[5] *Ibid.*
[6] Jürgen Habermas, "Civil society and the political public sphere", *Between Facts and Norms* (Cambridge: The MIT Press, 1996), pp. 329–387.

culture and thus, hegemony is manufactured, contested, negotiated and, finally, maintained.[7] Civil society, thus, becomes the "sphere of culture in the broadest sense" and is where values and meanings are contested, shaped and changed.[8] Viewed through Gramscian lenses, civil society provides the essential space through which both hegemonic and counter-hegemonic discourses take place. The Singaporean state's approach towards civil society is undeniably shaped by Gramscian lenses and is essentially Janus-faced. On one hand, it actively advocates an active citizenry through a vibrant civic society and understands this as a means of extending hegemony. On the other hand, it remains suspicious and, sometimes, seeks to manage the growth of an active autonomous civil society which it sees as a potential space for counterhegemonic discourse.

A Vibrant "Civic Society"

The Singapore government has often advocated the proliferation of a "civic society" over that of a civil society. The term first found articulation in 1991, by the then Acting Minister of Information and the Arts, George Yeo, who called for the creation of a "Singapore Soul" by an active citizenry, with an emphasis on the responsibilities to the nation. In another speech at a conference on civil society in 1998, Yeo mooted the notion of the "Singapore Idea" and expressed hope that there would be found "new and better ways to bind state and society together". The emphasis, it may be discerned, is on citizen participation that works within governmental and institutional frameworks rather than outside it. In Singapore, this has manifested in a focus on aspects such as good governance, civic responsibility, honesty, strong families, hard work, a spirit of voluntarism and a deep respect for racial and religious diversity. The result has been the flourishing of organisations such as the People's Association (PA), Community Centres (CCs) and Resident Committees (RCs), which are

---

[7] Antonio Gramsci and Joseph A. Buttigieg, *Prison Notebooks* (New York: Columbia University Press, 1992).
[8] Krishan Kumar, "Civil society: An inquiry into the usefulness of an historical term", *The British Journal of Sociology*, 44(3), 1993, pp. 375–395.

essentially civic groups that function as assistants to the state and perform important roles such as the provision of social services. Civic organisations such as the PA do play a key role in Singapore society — however, this has also meant that traditionally speaking, civic society and not civil society has flourished here.

Grounds for Wariness

Why has the Singapore government maintained a distinct wariness towards the development of a vibrant and potentially politically active civil society? Its suspicions, it may be argued, date back to the colonial days when an active civil society was a hotbed for communist organisations. Colonial Singapore possessed a highly vibrant civil society, set in the landscape of world wars, anti-colonial movements and a colonial state that was often absent with regards to welfare provision. Many of these were community-based organisations aimed at self-help.[9] The Chinese community had numerous trade and clan associations which offered a range of services to Chinese immigrants, including the building of schools and hospitals.[10] The Malay community benefitted from basic welfare provision from the British government but also formed self-help groups targeted at alleviating poverty.[11] Within the Tamil community, there were ideologically driven reform movements such as the Tamil Reform Association (TRA) that systematically targeted caste prejudices and poverty and helped raise education levels among the Tamil labour community in Singapore.[12]

Incidents such as the Hock Lee bus strike and riots of 1955, which were orchestrated by politically motivated trade unions and students, left

---

[9] Suzaina Kadir, "Singapore: Engagement and autonomy within the political status quo", in Muthiah Alagappa (ed.), *Civil Society and Political Change in Asia* (Minneapolis: Graywolf Press, 2016), pp. 328–329.

[10] Diane K. Mauzy and Robert Stephen Milne, *Singapore Politics Under the People's Action Party* (London: Routledge, 2002), p. 158.

[11] *Ibid.*

[12] Pravin Prakash, "Dravidian-Tamil-Indian: Language, identity, reform and progress in Singapore", Paper Presented at The Singapore Tamil Youth Conference, Singapore, 2014, pp. 12–19.

a deep impression on early People's Action Party (PAP) leaders. The PAP's own political struggle with left-leaning organisations in the 1960s and 1970s also taught it the potential dangers of politicised trade unions. After it came to power in 1959 and consolidated power through the 1960s, the PAP government moved swiftly to fill up most of the space that had hitherto been occupied by an active civil society.[13] This was achieved through a crackdown on left-wing organisations and a co-optation of trade unions.[14] The PAP created and strengthened its own grassroots organisations and actively and efficiently took over much of the welfare provision offered by communal civil society groups. The establishment of government-led self-help groups like MENDAKI (for the Malays), Singapore Indian Development Association (SINDA) (for the Indians) and the Chinese Development Assistance Council (CDAC) (for the Chinese) essentially curtailed the functionality of these autonomous civil society groups who could not compete with the state both in terms of resources or efficiency. The PAP further sought to regulate the autonomy of civil society groups through the Registrar of Societies and the regulations stipulated by the Societies Act, and occasionally employed the coercive arm of the state when it was deemed necessary.[15] Through the twin strategies of coercion and co-optation, the PAP has managed to effectively stifle the autonomy of civil society organisations in Singapore. A perusal of recent world history tells us that the government's fears are not completely unfounded. A politicised civil society holds the potential to be disruptive and violent, capable of causing extensive damage. A paternalistic approach to civil society has avoided such excesses. Increasingly, however, it is being debated whether in a globalised and increasingly politically aware Singapore, such an approach is feasible and, if indeed, it is time for policies on civil society to evolve in the context of Singapore's betterment?

---

[13] Diane K. Mauzy and Robert Stephen Milne, *Singapore Politics Under the People's Action Party*.

[14] Bilveer Singh, *Understanding Singapore Politics* (Singapore: World Scientific, 2017), pp. 96–99.

[15] Suzaina Kadir, "Singapore: Engagement and autonomy within the political status quo", p. 329.

An Evolving Political Culture and the Role of the Internet

The political culture in Singapore has undergone significant changes. The 2011 general election appears to have ushered in a more politically charged and aware citizenry that is determined to voice its concern, disapproval and opinions on social and political issues. The government seems to be increasingly aware of the shifting sands and has made efforts to engage the population in ways it had often shied away from in the past. In 2004, Prime Minister Lee Hsien Loong articulated that "the Government of Singapore will not view all critics as adversaries. If it is a sincere contribution to improve government policies … (we will) encourage the critic to continue to stay engaged or even counter argue."[16] In an interview with *The Washington Post* in 2013, the Prime Minister commented that: "It's a different generation, a different society, and the politics will be different. ... We have to work in a more open way."[17] Recent initiatives such as Our Singapore Conversation have been both lauded and criticised in equal measure. Many have called it a step towards more political engagement while others think it a mere talk-shop. What is clear, however, is that increased engagement must take place within carefully calibrated "liberalised" spaces under the clear observation of the space.

However, it must be acknowledged that the role of technology makes these expectations increasingly hard to maintain. An increasingly progressive political citizenry has been aided by the effects of globalisation and the popularity of social networking. The proliferation of ideas and opinions can no longer be contained within state boundaries. Cyberspace has continued to function as a space for alternative news sources and sociopolitical discussions. Social networking sites such as Facebook and Twitter have become hotbeds for discussion on political and social issues. Many civil society groups and activists have depended on the Internet to

---

[16] Lee Hsien Loong, "Building a civic society", Speech at the Harvard Club of Singapore's 35th Anniversary Dinner, 2004 (United Nations Public Administration Network), http://unpan1.un.org/intradoc/groups/public/documents/apcity/unpan015426.pdf.

[17] Lally Weymouth, "An interview with Singapore Prime Minister Lee Hsien Loong," *The Washington Post*, 15 March 2013, https://www.washingtonpost.com/opinions/an-interview-with-singapore-prime-minister-lee-hsien-loong/2013/03/15/5ce40cd4-8cae-11e2-9838-d62f083ba93f_story.html.

deepen and orchestrate the socio-political discourse in Singapore.[18] The state, through legislation, has, since the 1990s, strived to manage political discussions on the Internet with limited success. In recent years, heightened fears over the adverse effects of fake news sites and disinformation campaigns have made the regulation and supervision of cyberspace a greater priority than ever before.[19] The Protection from Online Falsehoods and Manipulation Bill was then introduced in parliament on April 1, 2019, underwent a second reading on May 8, assented by the president on June 3, and gazzetted on June 25.

The government must become acutely aware that in this new normal, issues and policies will be actively debated and thrashed out, regardless of legislation. It must take measures to promote more debate in public spaces between the citizens and itself, even as such exchange currently does take place via several avenues. Discussion and debate must entail all sides being open to the idea of learning from one another and willing to see the other's perspective. Otherwise, a culture where debate takes place without the government will become the norm. This culture promises an increasing reality of a digital society: online avatars engaged in what borders on mudslinging and hate. Civic society for all its positive social benefits cannot engage these opinions effectively but an active and vigorous civil society can. In an increasingly online world, there must be a culture of political engagement that is mature, educated and engaged for positive change.

A vibrant civil society and a capable government, plugged into one another, drawing from one another's strengths, can be a socio-political force of immense capabilities that Singapore should utilise. Political openness and evolution must be a gradual and two-way process, even in the face of mounting frustration. In many states, a swift and passion-fuelled political change have often resulted in fractured states with little benefit from the process. It is also imperative that this process is a two-way one, negotiated by both an open-minded government and an equally

---

[18] Suzaina Kadir, "Singapore: Engagement and autonomy within the political status quo", p. 347.

[19] Lee Li Ying, "Bill on deliberate online falsehoods could be tabled by first half of 2019: Edwin Tong," *Channel NewsAsia*, 27 December 2018, https://www.channelnewsasia.com/news/singapore/edwin-tong-bill-on-deliberate-online-falsehoods-11065190.

accommodating civil society. This is often a laborious process, especially given that our civil society is in many ways still in its infancy. The state, too, must shift its perspective, from a paternalistic approach to that of a mentor, more experienced and yet trusting of its protégé's capabilities. This becomes all the important as the state is also in the process of building a nation, and where the constituents are highly diverse.

The expansion of space for participatory politics in Singapore in the last few decades has necessarily not been vertical, targeted at diversifying or diluting political power at the top. Instead, it has been an incremental horizontal growth aimed at fostering diverse views and advocating change through bottom-up mobilisation. This augmentation of space has perhaps been most observable in the experiences of civil society groups like the Association of Women for Action and Research (AWARE) and the Nature Society Singapore (NSS) which offer enlightening examples of being successful in challenging entrenched traditional attitudes within the public sphere and lobbying the government to enact change.[20]

Both organisations took advantage of the greater opportunities for consultation that were offered by the Goh Chok Tong administration in the 1990s with the civic society project and managed to retain their autonomy while engaging in active advocacy *vis-à-vis* the government. The experiences of AWARE and National Council of Social Service (NCSS) suggest that despite the suspicions of the state, there is room for advocacy politics in Singapore and civil society groups can negotiate, manoeuvre and even broaden space for participatory citizenship.[21] The most observable successful strategy seems to involve a strict insistence on autonomy (thereby keeping its constituents contented) while working closely with the state on particular issues that relate closely to its speciality. Adopting an

---

[20] Constance Singam, "When ordinary people do extraordinary things", in Constance Singam and Margaret Thomas (eds.), *The Art of Advocacy in Singapore* (Singapore: Ethos Books, 2017), pp. 6–7. For a deeper understanding of the strategies used by AWARE, please refer to the chapter in the same book by Corinna Lim, pp. 306–317. A further analysis of the Nature Society's experiences and strategies is also available in the chapter in the same book by Ho Hua Chew and Shawn Lum, pp. 75–96.

[21] Chua Beng Huat, "The relative autonomies of the state and civil society", in Gillian Koh and Ooi Giok Ling (eds.), *State-Society Relations* (Singapore: Eastern University Press for Institute of Policy Studies, 2003), pp. 68–73.

antagonistic posture or embracing identity politics (especially with regards to race and religion) almost always attracts a swift condemnation and crackdown. This is largely because the PAP government understands the need to engage with civil society but will insist on dictating the pace and scope of engagement. This has often manifested in the state keeping possessive control on the electoral and identity politics while displaying a willingness to partially loosen its grip on the realm of conservatory, welfare and other social activities.[22]

Activists thus constantly must negotiate a tightrope of out-of-bound markers and a suspicious paternalistic state. Civil society advocacy in Singapore thus necessarily does not entail confronting or undermining the state. Instead it involves petitioning and pressuring the state to tackle ubiquitous citizenship concerns such as heritage preservation, environmental conservation, welfare provision and gender inequality. A cautious approach is also essential to ensure protecting the limited space afforded to participatory politics and advocacy from further incursion from the state. Civil society groups thus largely understand that rather than trying to effect fundamental and widespread change, it is better off urging the Leviathan to prudently prune the banyan tree.

The Making of a Political Nation in Singapore

Here, drawing from Aristotle, the concept of a political community is almost akin to metapolitics, namely, understanding the relationship and linkages between the state and the individuals within it, especially citizens. In this regard, the most important concept that relates to the rise of a political community is the quest for nation building. This is especially important for new, post-independent states, something that has also occupied Singapore's attention since it began its journey of political self-government in the late 1950s and particularly since August 1965 as an independent state.

Nation building has been of great importance for Singapore due to its short span of sovereign statehood, its past history being coloured by racial

---

[22] Suzaina Kadir, "Singapore: Engagement and autonomy within the political status quo", p. 349.

tensions and social unrest, and its geopolitical location of a largely Chinese majority state in what is described as a "Malay World". To promote national unity, building a political nation, promoting a national identity amongst its diverse people, with a buy-in to the concept of Singapore as a nation-state, has been part of Singapore's road to its existential survival. As Singapore is not a homogenous state, be it from the perspective of race, religion, language, culture and even past origins, the political elites adopted a multipronged approach through the concept of "Singaporean Singapore". This was to ensure that through national policies of social equality and mobility based on meritocracy, a sense of nationalism and national belonging could be imbued in its diverse people. The government, mainly the PAP, that has been in power since 1959, experimented with various approaches to construct the "imagined community" called a Singapore Nation.

In this regard, multiracialism and multiculturalism were and remain the key pillars of Singaporean society. The tone of nation building was clearly set by Lee Kuan Yew, Singapore's first prime minister, when he announced on 9 August 1965, on the republic's first day as an independent state, of the type of state Singapore would be: "We are going to be a multiracial nation in Singapore. We will set an example. This is not a Malay nation; this is not a Chinese nation; this is not an Indian nation. Everyone will have his place, equal: language, culture, religion".[23] Since then, this has been adopted as the basic philosophy of governance in Singapore. The basic idea is to give equal status to all ethnic, racial and religious groups regardless of race, creed or size. Each race is separate but equal. The need to maintain racial harmony among the various races and cultures is viewed as critical for peace and development. This is because the Singapore society is fundamentally diverse and pluralistic, resembling a "salad bowl", where many different cultures, despite being tossed together, still retain their individual identities while contributing to one distinctive main culture.[24] The *Singapore rojak*, be it Chinese, Indian or

---

[23] See Lee Hsien Loong's National Day Message on 8 August 2015. Available at https://www.pmo.gov.sg/national-day-message-2015.
[24] John Clammer, *Race and State in Independent Singapore, 1965–1990: The Cultural Politics of Pluralism in a Multi-Ethnic Society* (UK: Ashgate, 1998), pp. 71–87.

Malay, is a useful metaphor that conveys the essence of what drives Singapore's politics and characterises its political culture.

The policy of multiculturalism continues to be emphasised by the government to ensure stable intra-societal relations. Through various policies and deliberations, it aims to cultivate a sense of national identity. This is to ensure that regardless of race or religion, Singaporeans will be rooted to the republic with a strong sense of loyalty. This has become all the more challenging as the forces of globalisation have exposed Singaporeans to a vast array of competing cultures, values and lifestyles, many of which have diluted the sense of belonging to Singapore and what it stands for.

Singapore society is composed of four races: Chinese (75.18%), Malays (13.62%), Indians (8.84%) and Eurasians and others (2.36%). Within these major racial groups, there are further differences based on dialect and language. All these contribute to making Singapore's society extremely diverse, with distinct fault lines. To promote racial harmony and integration within society while allowing each race or ethnic group to retain and promote its unique characteristics and values, a two-pronged policy is pursued by the government. This entails the promotion of self-help and leadership by the communities, on the one hand, and policies that emphasise meritocracy and equality for all races, on the other.

Various policies have been put in place to foster and engender as a sense of nationhood, in the hope of creating a unique national political community in the context of Singapore. *Inter alia*, nation-building policies have been implemented along a broad spectrum to ensure national unity, a sense of equality while ensuring that the highly pluralistic communities develop a sense of togetherness.

At the political level, ensuring an effective government has been a key in this regard, ensuring that national policies are fairly implemented towards all Singaporeans. More important, specific policies have been implemented to ensure a sense of equality and representation in all key institutions of the state. Among others, these include, the introduction of the Group Representation Constituencies, almost tweaking the one-man-one-vote system to ensure that all minorities are represented in Parliament and the appointment of minorities as Presidents of the republic with five of the presidents from 1965 to the present, coming from minority communities, namely, Yusof Ishak, Benjamin Sheares, Devan Nair, S. R. Nathan and

Halimah Yacob. In 2017, the government even changed the constitution to ensure that there will always be a president from the minority. According to Prime Minister Lee Hsien Loong, the hiatus-triggered model means that while presidential elections will be open to candidates of all races, but if there is not a President from a particular community for five consecutive terms, then the next term will be reserved for a President from that community. This means that in the course of six terms, there should be at least one President from the Chinese, Malay, Indian and other minority communities, provided qualified candidates appear. For the 2017 presidential election, it was reserved for a candidate from the Malay community.[25]

Since independence, the government has also established the Presidential Council for Minority Rights and since the rise of racial and religious issues worldwide, including radicalisation, put in place institutions such as the Maintenance of Religious Harmony Act, the Inter-Racial and Religious Confidence Circles, and paid special attention to the importance of the Inter-Religious Organization that was first established in March 1949. Underpinning all these political measures is the belief that the best and brightest should be rewarded to hold the top positions in the republic. This is the near single-minded belief in the virtues of meritocracy, where an individual is to be rewarded, not based on race or religion but on his or her abilities. While this has courted some controversies, especially those who have failed to make it on a continuous basis with generation after generation condemned to the "lower class", still this is the best that Singapore has developed, with pressures mounting for merit to be determined not just by educational performance but also other measurements. Still, meritocracy has served Singapore well and largely accounts for the colour-blind character of Singapore, especially of its key office holders.

At the social-cultural level, many multiracial-oriented policies have been implemented to deflect the claim that Singapore is a "Chinese State". Among others, these policies include: the adoption of Malay as the National Language and English as the working language in Singapore, the practice of educational bilingualism with every child required to master

---

[25] See "Next presidential election to be reserved for Malay candidates: PM Lee", *The Straits Times*, 8 November 2016.

the English Language and a Mother Tongue, the practice of religious freedoms, the establishment of grassroots organisations that bring together citizens, especially in the housing estates where 80% of Singaporeans live, the establishment of ethnic self-help groups such as MENDAKI, SINDA, CDAC and the Eurasian Association, the multilingual mass media and broadcasting policies, public housing, National Service and constant launch of national campaigns to promote national policies. Equally critical in this regard are the economic policies to ensure that no Singaporean is left behind, with the government's policies aimed at sharing the national wealth with the disadvantaged citizens through a host of regularised and *ad hoc* measures.

Finally, there is also the legal dimension aimed at ensuring that no one will wreck the racial and religious peace in Singapore. With strong military and police in place, the government has also put in place strong laws, such as the Internal Security Act, Sedition Act and most recently, laws to prevent the circulation of fake news that can undermine national unity and ethnic peace in Singapore, be it from within or without. In the end, through a combination of these measures, it aims to, first, deter and prevent inter-racial and inter-religious violence that had broken out in the past in Singapore or elsewhere, and second, to build a nation out of disparate Singaporeans, as the only home that they belong to and one that is successful.

Conclusion

By any measure, Singapore's political community, at the universal level, is still in the process of construction and hence, it being described as a "nation-in-being". Despite being a new and highly pluralistic state, ethnic peace and harmony are highly cherished goals of the populace. Common experiences in schooling, housing, National Service and the work place, as well as awareness of what domestic conflicts have led to elsewhere, have led to a strong commitment to social, ethnic and religious peace. While the challenge of globalisation and rising ethnic and religious assertiveness have led to increasing consciousness and even, ethnonationalism, these have never been allowed to threaten domestic peace.

However, a number of emerging social and economic issues affect the pursuit of good life, especially when the drives are affected by the dictates of the market that has been prevalent in the last 60 years. Compounded by these changes, the rise of interest groups in the community has made the contemporary market situation more challenging. As such, the rise of the free market without measured policy interventions can lead to the widening of social divide. The solution of equality of outcome is not a panacea to deal with the matter as a number of multifactorial factors account for the situation. More importantly, early interventions measures such as at the personal, health, social psychosocial well-being, education, skills, economic and ecological levels, should be considered and a close follow-up of family and individual development can be pursued.

More early intervention programmes to enhance the educational and skills abilities beginning as early as possible will help individuals to move up the social and economic ladder. In view of the rising stratification of society, the early intervention in the child's education can assist in a more "equal" society in the coming years, especially where education is such an important determinant of one's future in a highly competitive society.

At the same time, due to the growing political maturity of Singapore, the emphasis on ethnic self-help groups has not widened the racial divide in the republic. This is because through a strategy of strengthening the "elements" to solidify the "whole", the sense of nationhood has been effectively promoted. Even though Singapore is still not a nation, its sense of nationhood has been strengthened and is growing day by day. Compared to the legacy of the British colonialists, through concerted measures by the political leadership since the late 1950s, Singapore has emerged as a nation and the sense of nationalism is growing, representing the arrival of a political community, with the attachment of the Singapore state as its cherished goal.

While Singapore's well-being will always be a work-in-progress, the young must also learn that any disruptive activities not in the interest of the common good will cause serious dis-welfare to Singapore.

Chapter 3

Mobilising Volunteers in Community Development

Francesca Phoebe Wah

Introduction

Three years ago, I had a desire to bless 120 children from Pasir Panjang Hill Community Services with soft toys on Children's Day. Yet, as an undergraduate, I did not have the financial ability to bless all children. I started asking my friends if they would like to contribute. Not only did they agree to contribute, they also spread the word to their friends. Within two days, I had sufficient funds to purchase soft toys for 364 children from four different social service agencies. Now, that is three times my initial target. Had I expected this? Clearly not! From this incident, one thing I am certain of is that we have people who care and are willing to give to those in need. There are resources in the community. But we need to mobilise and coordinate the giving efforts, be it giving in the form of money or time.

To make serious differences in the community, agencies need to involve a significant number of volunteers to work on the community needs in significant ways. Volunteerism is on its way to becoming a "norm" in one's professional identity as there is a growing interest from professionals to apply their skills for good.[1] Besides involving volunteers, it is equally important to coordinate their giving efforts. Hence, mobilising volunteers in community development entails engaging volunteers effectively and sustaining their passion for the community. This chapter aims to share some good practices for mobilising volunteers in community development.

Who Can Be a Volunteer?

Everyone. Everyone can make a difference. Every helping hand from each member of the community, regardless of age or background, counts in making the little but crucial difference in the life of another. The key lies in matching the skills and interests of the volunteer to the volunteering assignment. The next question would be, who does the matching? Well, a volunteer manager. To the best of my knowledge, most organisations do not have a dedicated volunteer manager. Ironically, organisations that lack manpower and resources rely more heavily on volunteers to accomplish their missions.

Roles of a Volunteer Manager and Potential Contributions to the Organisation

According to McCurley and Lynch, a volunteer manager performs the following three crucial tasks in an organisation:

(a) helps top management identify needed expertise,
(b) secures management support for volunteer efforts,
(c) oversees volunteers and manages the volunteers' activities to ensure voluntary efforts connect with the organisation's strategic goals.[2]

Similar to that of a human resource manager, a volunteer manager looks first into the needs and requisites of an organisation and then looks for volunteers to fill those roles. With intentional planning and vision setting,

---

[1] Robert J. Rosenthal, *Volunteer Engagement 2.0 Ideas and Insights Changing the World*, 1st edn. (New York: John Wiley & Sons Inc., 2015).
[2] Steve McCurley and Rick Lynch, *Volunteer Management: Mobilizing all the Resources of the Community*, 2nd edn. (Kemptville, Ontario: Johnstone Training and Consultation, 2006).

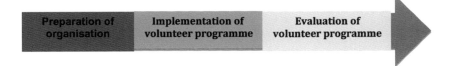

Figure 1. Volunteer programme design processes.

an effective volunteer manager can maximise volunteer participation by tapping effectively on the diverse interests and resources of volunteers. Hence, the first step to effective mobilisation of volunteers in community development is to employ a dedicated volunteer manager to direct and coordinate volunteering efforts. Figure 1 outlines the processes involved in designing a volunteer programme. A productive volunteer manager effectively manages these processes to maximise the value of volunteers to meet both the needs of the volunteer and organisation.

Preparation of Organisation

Recruiting volunteers is challenging these days and retaining volunteers is equally challenging. Retention begins even before recruitment. Retention requires preparation of the organisation to welcome volunteers. First, ensure sufficient financial support for the volunteer programme. One of the common myths is that volunteers are free. The truth is that there are several hidden costs in running a good volunteer programme in the community. As volunteers are major resources to Bringing Love to Every Single Soul (BLESS), it is crucial to ensure that sufficient resources are allocated to support volunteers. Costs need to be set aside for recruitment, training and appreciation.

Second, set a positive organisation climate. A good organisation climate is key to increasing retention rates. A clear sense of individual roles between volunteers and staff, mutual trust characterised by tolerance and acceptance, and open and honest communication gives volunteers a positive emotional experience in the work. Positive relationships with staff members contribute to volunteer retention.

Third, develop a support structure to nurture the contributions of volunteers. The agency also needs to take steps to institutionalise participation. McCurley and Lynch outline six principles for effective implementation and maintenance of citizen involvement efforts within the organisation, which are as follows:

1. Volunteers shall be involved in the organisation's service delivery system.
2. Volunteer programme shall have representation at the organisation's general management and administration level.
3. Volunteers provide both direct and indirect services.
4. Professional staff and volunteers shall be involved collectively in the planning and implementation of volunteer programme.
5. All aspects of volunteer programme will be monitored and evaluated at an ongoing basis.
6. Volunteers are regarded as non-paid staff, working in conjunction with professional staff to benefit the community.[3]

It is crucial to ensure that all levels of the organisation (from Board to Management Committee) are prepared and ready to work with volunteers for community development before embarking on a volunteer programme.

Implementation of a Volunteer Programme

Figure 2 outlines an overview of the volunteer management processes for the implementation of a volunteer programme.

Recruitment of Volunteers

While retention is an outcome, recruitment is a task. Retention happens with successful recruitment strategies that involve careful screening and thoughtful matching of volunteers. Effective recruitment starts with understanding the volunteer. Learn what each volunteer wants from their experience and what they can offer. Understanding motivations is crucial in recruitment. When volunteers' circles of needs are congruent with what

---

[3] *Ibid.*

Mobilising Volunteers in Community Development 39

Figure 2. Volunteer management processes.

Table 1. Why do people volunteer?

Personal motivations	Social motivations	Economic motivations	Community motivations
• To maintain skills no longer used otherwise • To fulfil a moral or religious duty • To gain new skills • To pay back • To assuage guilt • To feel useful • To try new challenges	• To have fun • To make new friends • To spend quality time with family/ friends by volunteering together	• To be part of a prestigious group • To meet important people in the community • To gain status • To gain work experience to help get a job • To make business contacts	• To gain knowledge of community problems • To help people • To improve community

the community needs and the organisation wants, it increases their satisfaction level. With a win–win situation for both volunteers and non-profits, there will be better volunteer retention rates.

Think about why you would want to volunteer? Table 1 shows some reasons why a volunteer volunteers.

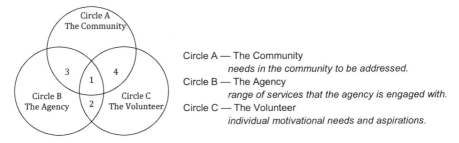

Figure 3. Motivational circles.

The three circles illustrated in Figure 3 show the primary motivational circles with which a volunteer programme is concerned, from the perspectives of the community, the agency and the volunteer.

Success lies in putting the circles together to maximise the ability of each participant to achieve their motivational needs. Let us examine the overlaps. Each of the four numbered areas represents something for the volunteer manager to consider.

(a) Overlap 1: Perfect Match

- The community has an area of need which falls within the type of services offered by the agency, which also falls within the motivational range of a volunteer.
- Volunteers can satisfy their own needs while contributing directly to the agency and the community.
- *Example*: Mentoring programme.

(b) Overlap 2: Still a Good Match

- There is an overlap between the motivations of the agency and the volunteer.
- However, satisfaction level of volunteers reduces when volunteers start to feel that they are not benefitting the community. Hence, it is crucial for the volunteer manager to continuously demonstrate to volunteers that they are contributing to meeting the needs.
- *Example*: Collecting information from the community for needs assessment.

(c) Overlap 3: A Slice of Potential

- The agency has a programme addressing the community needs but the programme does not match the volunteers' needs.
- Volunteer manager can consider possible expansion of the volunteer programme and redesign the volunteering assignment to meet volunteer's needs. Alternatively, they could also look into recruiting other volunteers with matching needs.

(d) Overlap 4: A Potential Partnership

- There is an overlap between the volunteer's motivations and community needs. However, the agency does not have a programme to address those needs.
- Volunteer manager can consider working with volunteers to design a new programme to address the community needs.

Everyone has different strengths. When enlisting the help of volunteers, agencies should also work to understand the individual's skill sets to ascertain where their time and service would be of the most value. For example, those who are strong in data entry can be used at the non-profit headquarters while those who are well-versed in customer service can help with outreach efforts. With diverse volunteers' interests and resources, properly identifying and then classifying volunteers based on skill can deliver results that are consistently positive and beneficial to the organisation.

Recruitment strategy #1: Publicise volunteer programme strategically

There are three crucial steps to publicise a volunteer programme: (a) explain what is in it for the volunteers, (b) offer a clear call to action and (c) make clear, achievable requests from them.

One should communicate the following to the volunteers:

1. Why should this work be done?
2. What will the benefit be to the community?
3. What are some possible fears or objections?
4. What will be the personal benefits to volunteers?

Figure 4. Recruitment strategies and platforms.

Each message identifies the specific needs, the ways in which a volunteer can address the needs and the benefits to the volunteer. The recruitment message should be inviting and encourage people to become involved.[4] To better engage and reach out to the target audience, different platforms are used. Figure 4 summarises the proposed strategies and platforms of recruitment to reach out to each type of target audience.

Recruitment strategy #2: Crafting volunteer job designs carefully

Job designs ought to carefully consider the life stage and motivations of potential volunteers to increase retention rates. When volunteers work in a position they look forward to and want to do, it gives them a sense of ownership, greater authority to think and a sense of responsibility for the results, which therefore contributes to volunteer retention.

Selection of Volunteers

It is recommended for the volunteer manager to interview the volunteers to identify their fit with the organisation. The interview allows the volunteer manager to learn more about the person, with an ultimate intent to

---

[4] Scott C. Stevenson (ed.), *Motivating Volunteers: 109 Techniques to Maximize Volunteer and Productivity* (San Francisco: Josey Bass, 2011).

shaping work situation that will be satisfying to the volunteer and the agency. It also provides an opportunity to match a role with a prospective volunteer's needs or tailor a role to a potential volunteer's background, skills, interests or availability.[5]

At the end of the interview, the volunteer manager should have a better understanding of the following:

(a) To what extent does the volunteer have both an interest in a particular job and the necessary qualifications to perform that job?
(b) To what extent does the volunteer have other interests and abilities that might be used to create a different job for him/her?
(c) To what extent does the volunteer have a rightness for working well in a particular job environment?

It would also be beneficial to carry out secondary screening for those volunteers who potentially have close contact with vulnerable beneficiaries.[6] Relevant reference checks might be conducted to ensure the selected candidates possess the knowledge, skills and attitudes to lead and contribute effectively, and to ensure the candidates have an enriching experience. After the rigorous screening process, the volunteer manager can match the shortlisted volunteers to the appropriate positions. All internal applicants who are not shortlisted should be informed as soon as it is known that they were not selected. An email could be sent out to thank them for their interest, provide feedback and direct them to other volunteering opportunities within the organisation and/or to reapply the following year.

Orientation of Volunteers

Volunteers, like any newbies on a job, need an orientation session. They need to be guided and equipped to do an assigned task well. Orientation clarifies the relationship between the volunteers and organisation.

---

[5] Tracy Daniel Connors (ed.), *The Volunteer Management Handbook: Leadership Strategies for Success* (New York: John Wiley & Sons Inc., 2012).
[6] Peter M. Kettner, *Excellence in Human Service Organisation Management*, 2nd edn. (New York: Pearson Education Inc., 2013).

Orientation is also crucial to increase retention as it reduces discrepancy between volunteers' expectations and reality. An orientation will help volunteers see how their position fits within the context of the organisation.[7] By seeing how their tasks forward the mission of the organisation, volunteers will find meaning in tasks that otherwise might seem menial. As volunteers represent the organisation to the public, the more the volunteers know and understand about the nature of organisation's operations and the cause, the more they can contribute to public relations, marketing and advocacy.

Contracting of volunteers should take place during the orientation. Having a clear contract that states the expected commitment from volunteers and a statement of commitment from agency to volunteers is also crucial for risk management. For example, getting volunteers to understand the agency's policies on confidentiality and getting volunteers to abide by the regulations ensure that the clients' sensitive information is protected. With proper contracting and orientation, it also protects the organisation against liabilities.

Orientation strategy #1: Having a three-part orientation

Adapting from McCurley and Lynch, organisations can consider having a three-part orientation programme — cause, system and social, to ensure that everyone is aligned to the organisation.[8] Including a cause orientation will help volunteers to see how they are contributing to community development. Volunteers join your organisation because they believe in a particular cause your organisation is calling for. So, give volunteers reasons to be passionate about the cause.

A system orientation ensures volunteers are clear with the policies and procedures of the organisation. Different scenarios could also be used to engage volunteers in conversations of how to deal with the possible dilemmas they might face in their journey. A social orientation would be helpful to orientate the volunteers to the organisation's culture. An

---

[7] Steve McCurley and Rick Lynch, *Volunteer Management: Mobilizing all the Resources of the Community.*
[8] *Ibid.*

organisation's culture refers to shared assumptions, values and norms within an organisation.[9] Organisation culture can potentially exert its influence through shaping the thinking and behaviour of volunteers.[10]

Supervision and Training

Another aspect of volunteer management is to provide ongoing support to the volunteers through supervision and training. When people are giving their time, it is important to treat them with respect for the work that they are doing. Volunteer management is not about being an overseer. Instead, it is more advantageous to help people understand how their help is needed and hear from them what further support they require. Then, support them in their work by providing additional training and managing the overall intricacies of a particular project. With a supportive environment, volunteers who feel welcomed by the organisation and competent enough in their job would continue to serve, increasing the retention rate. With greater support from the agency to the volunteers, it maximises volunteers' participation.

Strategy #1: Promote competency through training

Training develops more confident and more competent volunteers, which helps to keep the organisation moving forward.[11] It is recommended for the volunteer coordinator to conduct pre-match and post-match training to increase the competency of volunteers. Volunteers are primarily motivated by opportunities to learn new skills.[12] Professional development courses give volunteers opportunities to grow on the job. A volunteer manager helps to put in place training and equipping sessions to keep volunteers coming back and nurture them into their roles.

---

[9] Edgar Henry Schein, *Organisation Culture and Leadership* (San Francisco: Jossey-Bass, 1992).
[10] Peter M. Kettner, *Excellence in Human Service Organisation Management*.
[11] Tracy Daniel Connors (ed.), *The Volunteer Management Handbook: Leadership Strategies for Success*.
[12] Robert J. Rosenthal, *Volunteer Engagement 2.0 Ideas and Insights Changing the World*.

Strategy #2: Promote accountability though supervision

Supervision for new volunteers would begin as soon as they join the organisation, and should continue on a regular basis throughout their stay. Regular supervision provides the opportunity for staff and volunteers to work out problems, get to know the organisation well and establish a good and productive relationship with their supervisor.[13] By the same token, it allows the supervisor to get a clear picture of volunteers' strengths and needs, lets them know how they are doing, helps them work on areas where they are not strong enough and praises them for what they do well.

The goal of supervision is to help the volunteers to do the best job they can and continue to learn and improve. Supervisors will take on two roles. First, a mentoring role, where supervisors provide helpful and constructive feedback, developing a good relationship with the new volunteer and working to continually improve the understanding of and competence as a volunteer.

Supervisors also take on an administrator role, wherein they are responsible for making sure that the volunteers do their jobs. Supervision sessions give the volunteer's supervisor a chance to talk about the volunteer's performance. It also gives volunteers a chance to discuss their job scope and suggest changes. Format of each supervision session should include a review of past performance, discussion about the present and plans for the future.

Strategy #3: Promote retention though creating an esteem-building climate

Creating an esteem-building climate — increasing connectedness, uniqueness and power — for volunteers is also crucial for volunteer retention. Engaging in new experiences together enhances people's sense of connectedness. Giving them challenging assignments that take advantage of their individual strength enhances people's sense of uniqueness. People's sense of power is enhanced when they get to work on things that matter to them. All of these contribute to a higher volunteer retention rate.

---

[13] Tracy Daniel Connors (ed.), *The Volunteer Management Handbook: Leadership Strategies for Success.*

Strategy #4: Promote participation though regular engagement

Volunteers are also motivated by opportunities to have a voice in the organisation. There should be regular feedback channels for volunteers to offer suggestions for improvements and volunteers should also be included in planning that might affect their work. Engaging the volunteer for ideas and decision-making also increases the retention rate. It allows volunteers to feel part of the team to accomplish the mission of the organisation. Volunteers feel special and recognised and are therefore motivated to work harder to contribute to the organisation and the community. Conduct regular dialogue sessions with volunteers to gather their feedback and implement their ideas selectively. This system builds loyalty and instils confidence in volunteers.

It is also important to stay tuned in to identify the volunteers' life cycles. The organisation and the volunteers are constantly evolving. Hence, a natural cycle of involvement typically exists between most organisations and their volunteers, and that the volunteer naturally becomes less active overtime. Realising the natural life cycle of volunteering, consider the following to ensure seamless transitions:

(a) determine the length of service for key positions;
(b) communicate with volunteers who are especially valuable;
(c) establish both long- and short-term responsibilities for each volunteer.

Recognition and Appreciation

The other aspect is to provide recognition of volunteers for their efforts. When volunteers have positive emotional experiences with the organisation, it develops their volunteer role identity. With a volunteer experience that meets the volunteers' motivational needs in ways that are productive for organisation and satisfying for the individual, it increases volunteers' retention rate and maximises volunteers' talents.

Recognising volunteers' contributions makes the volunteers feel valued by the organisation, thus increasing their motivation to continue to provide high-quality services.[14] Both formal and informal volunteer

---

[14] Scott C. Stevenson (ed.), *Motivating Volunteers: 109 Techniques to Maximize Volunteer and Productivity*.

Table 2. Motivating and hygiene factors.

Motivating factors	Hygiene factors
• Annual awards ceremony • Include volunteers in special events • Recommend volunteers to prospective employers/letters of reference • Celebrate achievements and milestones • Recognise and accommodate personal needs and problems	• Ensure volunteers' health and safety standards are not compromised • Keep volunteers informed about programme outcomes and updates via newsletters • Send birthday and greeting cards • Highlight outstanding youth volunteers on Special Youth Functions • Honour volunteers on International Volunteers Day

recognition strategies are employed to promote excellence amongst volunteers. Herzberg two-factor theory is used to design the volunteer recognition framework.[15] Examples of recognition strategies are outlined in Table 2.

There are key underlying principles across all recognition strategies. All recognition must be done in a personal and honest manner. If possible, recognition should be tailored to the unique needs of each volunteer to acknowledge them in ways appropriate to each individual. To ensure volunteers see a clear connection between accomplishments and recognition, volunteers should be recognised promptly and know why they are being recognised.

Evaluation of Volunteer Programmes

Evaluation is important as it adds credibility to the organisation and allows the volunteer manager to reflect on ways to better achieve the mission. Evaluation should include both programme and volunteer management programme. Inputs (resources used to meet volunteer programme

---

[15] Frederick Herzberg, "The motivation-hygiene concept and problems of manpower", *Personnel Administration*, 27, 1964, pp. 3–7.

goals), programme objectives (beneficiaries and volunteers), activities, outputs, outcomes and impacts form the evaluation grid.[16]

It is important for the leaders and decision-makers within the organisation to have a clear picture of the cost and benefits of volunteer programme. It uncovers how much of an investment is being made for the volunteer programme. Evaluation also helps volunteers to work closer to develop their potential and helps the organisation think of better ways to involve the volunteers. Regular evaluation allows for the development of a more robust volunteer management program. Sharing the impact of programme with volunteers also increases their retention rate.

Conclusion

Enlisting the help of volunteers in community development is just as important as raising money for the poor. Both are critical components to not only help a community survive, but also thrive. People are empowered as they gain a sense of personal efficacy through accomplishing their shared goals for the community. To do so, organisations need to have effective volunteer management practices to engage the public to contribute their time to serve others. No one can do everything, but everyone can definitely do something. Collectively, we can do much more.

---

[16] Catherine Alter and Susan Murty, "Logic modeling: A tool for teaching practice evaluation", *Journal of Social Work Education*, 33(1), 1997, pp.103–117.

Chapter 4

Neighbours Programme: A Community Work Approach to Integrate Health and Social Services for Acute Care Hospital Patients

Goh Soon Noi, Zahara Mahmood and Eugene Shum

Transformation of Healthcare

Healthcare in Singapore has been evolving. Beyond institution-based care, there has been increasing emphasis on healthcare integration and population-based care. In 2000, the healthcare system was organised into two clusters — SingHealth and National Healthcare Group — to bring about greater integration and coordination between hospitals, polyclinics and speciality centres. The healthcare system further evolved with the formation of six regional health systems (RHS) beginning in 2008. Each RHS was responsible for the population in a region. In addition to operating a range of healthcare institutions, each RHS had an important role to build partnerships among healthcare providers (non-governmental organisations (NGOs) and private organisations) in their respective region. These partnerships extended to healthcare organisations such as acute and community hospitals, primary care providers, nursing homes and other long-term care providers. It also included social service and community partners. This helped to shift healthcare from episodic to holistic patient care, from providing healthcare services to also keeping individuals in good health and from interventions at the individual level to also include systems-level interventions focusing on population health.[1]

In 2017, the Singapore Ministry of Health (MOH) announced further transformation required for a future-ready healthcare system with three fundamental foci. This was in light of the chronic disease burden, ageing population, declining workforce and challenging economic outlook. First, shifting beyond providing healthcare to promoting health upstream. Second, transforming a delivery system that is built around hospital-based care to community-based care. And third, moving beyond quality to value. The healthcare budget has more than doubled from S$4.7 billion in FY2012 to S$11 billion in FY2016, and the third focus is to ensure system sustainability.

There are many challenges in transforming the healthcare delivery system from hospital-based care to community-based care involving the social sector. The current model for providing health and social services in Singapore has been described as the mixed economy, otherwise known as the Many Helping Hands approach in the social care sector, consisting of a partnership between the government, the voluntary sector and the private sector.[2] For health services, primary care, acute general service and specialist services are largely provided by the public sector; intermediate and long-term care (ILTC) services are offered by voluntary welfare organisations (VWOs); and the private sector provides a range of these services. Having partnerships among organisations across health and social sectors and within each sector to ensure integration and care that is

---

[1] Eugene Shum and Lee Chien Earn, "Population-based healthcare: The experience of a regional health system", *Annals Academy of Medicine*, 43(12), 2014, pp. 564–565.

[2] Lim Meng-Kin, "Shifting the burden of health care finance: A case study of public-private partnership in Singapore", *Health Policy*, 69, 2004, pp. 83–92; K. K. Mehta and C. Briscoe, "National policy approaches to social care for elderly people in the United Kingdom and Singapore, 1945–2002", *Journal of Aging & Social Policy*, 16(1), 2004, pp. 89–112; Peggy Teo, Kalyani Mehta, Thang Leng Leng and Angelique Chan, *Ageing in Singapore: Service Needs and the State* (Oxon, Great Britain: Routledge, 2006).

client-centred is complex. The responsibility for delivering services to any individuals or groups lies with many agencies, each with its own funding mechanisms, budget, jurisdiction and criteria for client selection. As a result, there can be discontinuities in the service provision for the clients. Moreover, the development of the healthcare system is heavily inclined to an approach that is expert-driven, proprietary, top-down, planned and provider-focused. This is in contrast with the development of the social care sector which has incorporated client participation, client empowerment and the engagement of community through the community work method to provide care and support for clients.[3]

This chapter will discuss the concept of community work and how it has been applied locally in a healthcare setting. The case example presented will demonstrate the potential use of community work method to help hospitals work with the community partners to ensure patients' access to services and continuity of care.

How Community Work Is Relevant for the Healthcare Sector?

Research has shown that socio-economic factors affect health outcomes. Residents living in economically distressed communities are found to have higher health risks.[4] Cohen and his team found a relationship between the quality of housing in a neighbourhood and early deaths from diseases.[5] World Health Organization (WHO), in its definition of health, emphasises that social and economic conditions shape the health of individuals and communities. It is also the responsibility

---

[3] S Vasoo, "Community development in Singapore: New directions and challenges", *Asian Journal of Political Science*, 9(1), 2001, pp. 4–17.
[4] Robert J. Sampson, "The neighbourhood context of wellbeing", *Perspectives in Biology and Medicine*, 46, 2003, pp. S53–S64; Paula Braveman and L. Gottlieb, "The social determinants of health: It's time to consider the causes of the causes", *Public Health Reports*, 129(2), 2014, pp. 19–31.
[5] Deborah A. Cohen, Karen Mason, Ariane Bedimo, Richard Scribner, Victoria Basolo and Thomas A. Farley, "Neighborhood physical conditions and health", *American Journal of Public Health*, 93, 2003, pp. 467–471.

of governments to address health disparities, healthcare inequality and access to healthcare of their citizens.[6]

This approach to health takes on an interdisciplinary perspective that includes humanities, social sciences, clinical and population research, medical anthropology and sociology, public health, health economics and policy. It helps to better understand how social and economic conditions impact health, disease and the practice of medicine. Corollary to this, many of the patients' problems would suggest a complex array of individual-, family- and community-level factors that point to the need for additional community-level strategies to ameliorate their health problems. It is believed that a supportive community can mitigate the threats posed by risky environments.

It is in this context that community work as a method can help to extend the dimension of the analysis out of the micro-level, to address the systemic issues that underpin patients' problems. It "focuses on the ways in which peoples' physical and organisational environment furthers or hinders their well-being, and thereby promotes the interaction of individuals and groups living in the same community. The objective of community work is to enhance the capacity of the communities to promote social functioning by strengthening resources, services and opportunities to meet various life tasks, alleviate distress and realise aspirations and values".[7] Patients, particularly those with chronic diseases, disabilities and terminal conditions discharged from hospitals require both informal (families, friends, etc.) and formal (primary, ILTC and personal social services) support to ensure their adjustment and integration in their communities. When care and support in the community break down or are inadequate, patients' physical health may be affected. This results in frequent Accident and Emergency Department attendances and hospital admissions resulting in higher utilisation of hospital services. Therefore, the health sector needs to focus attention on the communities that patients return to and address

---

[6] World Health Organization. Downloaded on 18 October 2017 from https://en.wikipedia.org/wiki/World_Health_Organization#Health_policy.

[7] C. Briscoe, "Community work and social work in the United Kingdom", in H. Specht and A. Vickery (eds.), *Integrating Social Work Methods* (London: George Allen and Unwin, 1979), p. 183.

the social and environmental conditions to promote health and to prevent high utilisation of hospital services.

What Is Community Work?

Community work intervention uses community as the target. The main approach to this work is a belief that people acting together have a great capacity to improve their own circumstances, as they have first-hand knowledge of the situation and what needs to happen to change things for the better.

What then is "community"? McDonell and Melton's *community* refers to the sense of common interest among residents of a neighbourhood or any other geographic unit who are drawn together by emotional ties and social exchanges.[8] In a prior work, McDonell defined community as "a physical place and as content and process, or sets of activities within and across sectors of the community, and the norms, values, and beliefs guiding the activity".[9] In this sense, community is best understood in terms of its physical, social, political, economic and institutional/organisational dimensions, and the integration, collaboration and coordination among its various aspects relative to a resident's well-being. Each community is highly dynamic, constantly changing in response to internal and external forces. Community boundaries can change as changes in zoning regulations to alter land-use patterns or electoral boundaries. Leaders in the community change as new economic and social priorities emerge. The social issues affecting the lives of residents are embedded within and across the various dimensions of the community. When referring to characteristics of the community in question, such references are often associated with the demography, social, health and mental health problems present, and the issues of access to amenities, social services and health services.

---

[8] James R. McDonell and G. B. Melton, "Toward a science of community intervention", *Farm Community Health*, 31(2), 2008, pp. 113–125.

[9] James R. McDonell, "Indicator measurement in comprehensive community initiatives", in Asher Ben-Arieh and Robert M. George (eds.), *Indicators of Children's Well-Being: Understanding Their Role, Usage, and Policy Influence* (Dordrecht, Netherlands: Springer-Verlag, 2006), pp. 33–43.

A dimension related to community work is *community development*. There are different nuances to the definition of community development, but all embrace the basic concept of a process where community members come together to take collective action and generate solutions to common problems. The term is broad and can refer to the practices of civic leaders, activists, involved citizens and professionals to improve various aspects of communities, typically aiming to build stronger and more resilient local communities.

Community development seeks to empower individuals and groups of people with the skills they need to effect change within their communities. These skills are often created through the formation of social groups working for a common agenda. According to Estes, community development practice has always been at the conceptual centre of social work practice in urban areas for the following three reasons: (1) community work seeks to unite previously unorganised people into effective groups and coalitions that work together in pursuit of a shared social agenda (e.g. improved schools, safer neighbourhoods); (2) community work seeks to strengthen traditional family, kinship and neighbourhood ties in the community and to develop new social arrangements that are essential for the effective functioning of communities and (3) community-based social services are among the most effective and cost-effective approaches for serving the poor.[10]

Community development occurs when people organise themselves to develop long-term strategies for problem solving.[11] Estes pointed out that community development focuses on self-help and voluntary cooperation among members or residents of the disadvantaged communities or sectors of society.[12] It also strives to acquire or redistribute resources on behalf of the poor and marginalised social groups.[13] Typically, community devel-

---

[10] Richard J. Estes, "Social work, social development and community welfare centers in international perspective", *International Social Work*, 40, 1997, pp. 43–55.

[11] Herbert J. Rubin and Irene S. Rubin, *Community Organizing and Development* (New York: Macmillan, 1992).

[12] Richard J. Estes, "Social work, social development and community welfare centers in international perspective", pp. 43–55.

[13] Apollo Rwomire, "The role of social work in national development", *Social Work & Society International Online Journal*, 9(1), 2011.

opment targets local communities beset with economic and social problems, such as concentrations of poverty, high crime rates, abandoned buildings, substandard housing, outdated infrastructure, unemployment and a poor economy. The specific objectives of community development depend, however, not only on the needs of the local community but also on the interests of the organisation or group initiating the development activity. Jones insightfully pointed out the inherent contradiction in community development "where on one hand emphasized participation, initiatives and self-help by local communities but on the other hand is usually sponsored by national government as part of a national plan".[14]

Another dimension of community work is community organising. Community organising entails bringing people together to deal with shared problems and to increase their say about decisions that affect their lives. This approach also entails engaging in a broad range of social change activities, including advocacy with and on behalf of the community for reform of the underlying social, political and economic conditions that undermine human dignity. Community organisation addresses problems such as lack of affordable housing, drug abuse, discrimination and lack of access to healthcare.

In community development, community workers work in cooperation with the community to identify the needs and to develop or improve services and systems to meet those needs. In community organising, community workers endeavour to improve socio-economic systems and generate resources so that more people in the community will have access to the services they need to function at their best. They usually work for, or with, governmental, private or community organisations to determine community needs and to recommend and develop new resources.[15]

Community work has its focus on bringing about structural change in the community. It involves an understanding of the power dynamics and social relations that govern the relationships between the various

---

[14] D. Jones, "Community work in the United Kingdom", in H. Specht and A. Vickery (eds.), *Integrating Social Work Methods* (London: George Allen and Unwin, 1970), p. 171.
[15] http://www.social workers.org.

structures and diverse groups in the community.[16] Hence in community work, the worker has to spend much time working with the community leaders and allies to identify common goals among the stakeholders. The community worker shares information related to the presenting problem or issue so that the stakeholders are better able to participate in formulating solutions. If the issue is poverty, the community worker may focus on the societal and individual circumstances that create these conditions. This may include trying to address the policies that perpetuate poverty or organising groups around the issue to lobby decision-makers for change. The community worker often becomes the leading organiser to generate a strategic direction in the context of goals identified and defined by the group that the group will work towards. Through organising people to participate in this collective action of identifying needs of the community and solving community problems collectively, living environment and quality of life can improve. Some of the tools utilised by the community workers include developing community awareness, leadership identification and development, creating strategic alliances, adult education, fostering collaboration and building community capacity.

The case example will illustrate the community work method used to drive the programme.

A Case Example — Neighbours for Active Living Programme

The Neighbours for Active Living Programme or *Neighbours* was developed by Changi General Hospital (CGH)/Eastern Health Alliance (EHA),[17] the RHS for eastern Singapore and South East Community Development Council (SECDC). The programme integrates health and social expertise and resources in the respective communities to help frail seniors manage their health problems. It operates along a community work model. *Neighbours* was launched in July 2013 in the Bedok and

---

[16] J. Hall, "Social work practice in community development", Downloaded on 8 August 2017 from http://www.casw-acts.ca/en/social-work-practice-community-development.
[17] From 2018, due to MOH reclustering of the public health institutions, EHA ceased and CGH comes under the SingHealth cluster.

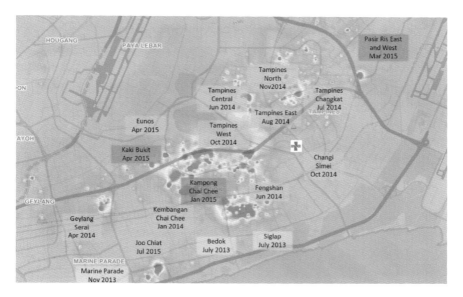

Figure 1. Scaling the Neighbours for Active Living Programme across the eastern region.

Siglap communities. By June 2015, the programme has expanded to a total of 18 communities covering the entire eastern region and served a total of 4,500 seniors with complex health and social care needs (Figure 1).

Neighbours comprises two arms — (a) a full-time Community Care Team from CGH involving professionals with health and social care expertise and (b) volunteers from the SECDC Friend-a-Senior programme. The CGH Community Care Team comprises more than 50 full-time staff who are professionals with nursing, social work, psychology and related training. They are sited full time within the local neighbourhood. The responsibilities of the Community Care Teams are to (a) understand the holistic care needs of seniors, (b) navigate and facilitate referral to services and (c) provide longitudinal tracking and long-term monitoring of clients. The CGH Community Care Team partners collaborate closely with formal services such as social support services, healthcare volunteer welfare organisations and informal networks such as grassroots leaders, volunteers and residents (Figure 2).

By 2017, over 450 volunteers have been trained by the CGH Community Care team. The two-day Friend-A-Senior training comprises

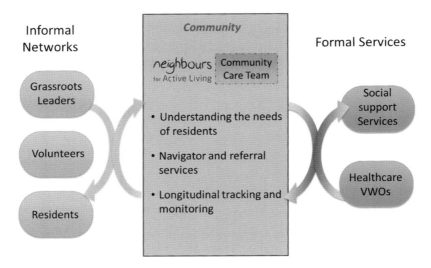

Figure 2. Partnership between the Community Care Team with formal services and informal networks.

communication, befriending skills and knowledge of chronic diseases and mental health issues. The volunteers come from various backgrounds ranging from homemakers to professionals. When the Community Care Team receives a referral, they visit the client to assess and work out the specific interventions. Once a client is found to be stable, the team matches the client with the volunteers.

The volunteers are matched to elderly clients living in the same local neighbourhoods. They provide social support and assist with simple but important tasks, such as reminding clients to take their medications and attend medical appointments. This enables the forging of long-term relationships that enable elderly residents to stay as healthy as possible where they live. Clients who need help are often frail and elderly and have a combination of needs beyond medical, for example, assistance with activities of daily living and caregiver support. The volunteers are supported by the CGH Community Care Team. If the volunteers identify any issues of concern, they can highlight it to the CGH professionals.

Prior to the introduction of the *Neighbours*, healthcare support for patients discharged from the hospital focused on the immediate post-discharge period. *Neighbours* was set up in line with the national direction to make healthcare support services ongoing rather than episodic especially for patients with long-term chronic conditions like diabetes, stroke, cancer, lung and heart diseases living in the community. The aim of the programme is to make each patient healthcare journey as hassle-free, assuring and convenient as possible, while educating, empowering and supporting the patients and caregivers to manage their health well, in order to live as healthy for as long as possible with the support from partners and individuals in the community.

Taking a Population-Based Perspective

As far back as 2012, CGH/EHA tapped on the geographic information system (GIS) and integrated the hospital databases including the Social Work Information System (SWIS) to frame its patients' conditions as well as the health problems in the community, determine the geographical spread of these problems, define the demography of the community residents with chronic diseases, as well as identify the issues related to access and patterns of utilisation of health and social services (Figure 3). Having a good understanding of the community ecosystem is also critical. The technology capability to generate spatial representations of neighbourhood data and to link information and resources within CGH/EHA enables the hospital to adopt a population-based lens to bring to bear on the community's most urgent problems as other institutions have demonstrated.[18]

In addition, CGH has long taken a "hospital without walls" perspective and already made many inroads into working and collaborating with the various stakeholders in the community.[19] The CGH knows and is known by many of the stakeholders in the communities where it is making its entry.

---

[18] Helen Rehr and Rosenberg Gary, *The Social Work-Medicine Relationship: 100 Years at Mount Sinai* (New York: The Haworth Press Inc., 2006).

[19] Goh Soon Noi and K. K. Tan, "Hospital without walls — Extending the care beyond hospital — A hospital-community coordinated care (HCC) project", in *The Proceedings of the 5th International Conference on Social Work in Health and Mental Health*, Hong Kong, 6 December 2006, pp. 10–14; Goh Soon Noi and Z. Mahmood, "Care transitions intervention for elderly patients with complex care conditions", Poster Presentation at The 6th MOH Clinical Quality Conference, Singapore, 2009; Melissa Pang, "Eastern Health Alliance — All-rounded care under one grouping. Eastern Health Alliance set up to provide integrated patient care", *The Straits Times*, 18 November 2011. Downloaded on 17 October 2017 from http://ifonlysingaporeans.blogspot.sg/2011/11/eastern-health-alliance-all-rounded.html.

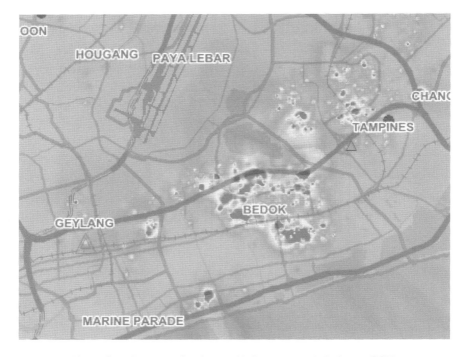

Figure 3. Hotspots of patients with frequent readmission to CGH.

Engaging and Forging Strategic Alliances

Early work involved meetings and sharing with the Community Development Councils (CDCs), mayors and community leaders to inform each other of the issues and concerns and explore how grassroots and community ecosystem can work with CGH/EHA to support its patients living in their communities. The aim is to develop a strategic partnership that allows both the health and social needs of patients/residents to be addressed comprehensively and in a more integrated and seamless manner. It resonates with SECDC, for at the helm is the mayor who steers efforts in achieving the three strategic thrusts that guide the work of CDC, termed the "ABCs of Community Bonding", which refer to assisting the needy, bonding the people and connecting the community. SECDC initiates and manages programmes in collaboration with both community and corporate partners along these three strategic thrusts, so as to nurture a vibrant and self-reliant community. Being a strong advocate for social services and playing a role of social broker, SECDC has also helped to promote *Neighbours* to all communities under the district.

The critical success factor in partner relations lies with the maintenance of close communication channels with its supporters like the Grassroots Advisors who are the community leaders in the various communities and the champions for driving collaboration at the local levels.

Bridging the Health and Social Divide

Neighbours target to address the health–social divide to deliver the continuum of services that patients/residents require. In Singapore, healthcare and social support come under separate government agencies. Service planning, funding, resourcing and delivery in turn tend to be separate. As a result, many of the services delivered are fragmented resulting in problems of access to these services.[20]

A key challenge of this programme is the paradigm shift from a traditional agency-led fixed service model approach to one which involves close partnerships with VWOs, health and social service organisations and other community organisations to deliver the critical services that patients/residents require. There are varying capabilities and service models in the community. Hence, there is a need to understand the uniqueness of each organisation and adapt the approach so that there is synergistic and complementary delivery of service. Instead of having competing overlapping services, this approach helps to minimise duplication and waste while ensuring that the service gaps are addressed.

The uniqueness of *Neighbours* — feature of community work — is bringing other organisations to the aid of its patients and also to complement and enhance services which these organisations provide. Invariably, it is not easy getting support from various stakeholders. Starting with a small pilot and gradually scaling up allow the programme to

---

[20] From 1 April 2018, oversight of social care services for frail seniors was transferred from the Ministry of Social and Family Development to MOH to enable MOH to integrate planning and policy-setting for health and social support services for seniors.

demonstrate early results and at the same time refining and enhancing the approach as it scaled.

Embedding the CGH Community Care Team in the Community

The programme is centred on the local community. The CGH Community Care Teams are embedded and sited full time in the 18 communities under the EHA service boundary, where they support residents living in the area and work closely with the organisations sited there:

(1) Southeast districts, namely Bedok, Siglap, Kembangan-Chai Chee, Kampong Chai Chee, Fengshan, Marine Parade, Geylang Serai, Joo Chiat and Changi-Simei.
(2) Northeast districts, namely Pasir Ris East, Pasir Ris West, Tampines Central, Tampines-Changkat, Tampines West, Tampines East, Tampines North, Eunos and Kaki Bukit.

Each CGH Community Care Team spends 80% of its time within the local community. Each team is accessible not only to patients/residents in the community but also to community partners. This enables the team to form close relationships with patients/residents and community agencies, and grassroots leaders and organisations. This is in contrast to the traditional approach where a team is located centrally in the hospital and deployed only when there is a service need. The close relationship that the CGH Community Care Team forms with the residents enables the team to truly understand the needs of patients/residents, respond to them in an appropriate and timely manner and deliver the support that they require. The partnership with community agencies and grassroots organisations allows for greater synergy and sustainability in providing long-term support for the residents.

Collaboration with Community Partners

Neighbours is a multi-partner, multi-agency, multi-organisation programme. The hallmark of this programme is the high level of flexibility and customisations on implementation at the local level. It is this synergistic and symbiotic approach that allows patients/residents despite their high health and social care needs to benefit from the respective organisations/providers.

There is a very strong community participation and ownership in this programme with close involvement of informal networks such as grassroots organisations and residents in the community. They are actively involved in driving and the delivery of the services. They also play an additional role in linking more partners and strengthening existing partnerships.

Participation through Volunteering to Complement the CGH Community Care Team

The Community Care Team is complemented by trained volunteers who support the residents under the *Neighbours* programme. The Friend-A-Senior and North-East Care Team volunteers supporting *Neighbours* in the 18 communities receive ongoing training and support from the CGH Community Care Team.

These volunteers are also neighbours of the residents requiring support. As more and more elderly persons live apart from their families, the concept of 远亲不如近邻 or neighbours helping neighbours becomes even more important.

The volunteers go beyond traditional befriending. They undergo a two-day structured training programme to prepare them for the role. The volunteers then form a team of three members under the group volunteering concept. Thereafter, the volunteers are matched with their neighbours based on their proximity, gender, language spoken, personality, experience and skills.

The involvement of fellow neighbours as volunteers has also helped to build community bonding and social capital. This group-volunteering approach is more sustainable and has allowed their befriendees to be supported on a long-term basis. The volunteers and community leaders who come on board to be part of the volunteer group also serve as "sensors" in the community for the CGH Community Care Team. They help to detect early problems or red flags and alert the CGH Community Care Team early to prevent unnecessary hospitalisations of the residents.

Impact and Value Creation of the **Neighbours** *Programme*

A study of 2,540 clients who were recruited from 2013 to 2016 under the *Neighbours* showed that over the six months that the clients were in the programme, their hospital readmission reduced by 55% from 2.2 to 1.0 admissions. This is a considerable impact as many of these clients were vulnerable, elderly residents with complex medical and social needs with frequent hospital readmission prior to enrolment in the *Neighbours*.

Challenges Encountered in the **Neighbours**

While the programme achieves provision of healthcare, social services and related support at the right time and right place to the right patients/residents, it is not without challenges. There exists a constant poor "fit" between the needs of the multi-problem patients/residents and existing infrastructure of therapeutic and personal care work. For example, the provision of the services required by these residents is the responsibility of many sectors (health — primary, acute, intermediate and long-term, social and housing), several jurisdictions (private, voluntary welfare, community and government) and numerous organisations, grassroots groups and informal groups. These various components of the therapeutic and personal care work seemingly existing in parallel have separate funding streams and budgets, resulting in frequently conflicting requirements and eligibility. What surfaces is that health and social care differ distinctively in terms of language, culture, professional roles and responsibilities, clinical and service approaches. Consequently, the biggest challenge is the coordination of the multiple stakeholders in defining the needs of the residents/community and the provision of an integrated and comprehensive service, so as to ensure a continuity of care that empowers the residents, their family carers and the community.

Fundamental Change Needed

The integration of multiple stakeholders requires a coherent set of methods of needs determination, intervention and models of funding, administrative, organisational and service delivery designed to create connectivity, alignment and collaboration within and between the cure and care work. While the programme sheds some light on the discontinuities and behoves the relevant organisations to act, the programme continues to push its boundary for patient/resident advocacy. While challenging, it is equally important to enhance system efficiency for patients/residents with complex, long-term problems cutting across multi-services, providers and settings. It has to be a bottom-up approach from a client-centric perspective.

Thus far in the healthcare sector, the level of patients'/residents' participation in need determination and decision-making on what and how services/programmes are delivered is limited. The healthcare sector will need to emulate and exploit the strength and resources in the social care sector to engage and empower patients/residents. This will ensure that the transformation of service delivery from hospital-based to community-based care is indeed the right care and the right place for the right patients/residents. Sustainability and transferability are key issues when evaluating a programme. Hybrids of the programme that take into account local, institutional and community variabilities are emerging as the programme progresses. They represent a growing continuum of health and social care as well as a reflection of the extent of community participation.

Looking Ahead

Many hospitals have various initiatives and programmes to promote health in the community. What is different in the *Neighbours* programme is the use of community work method to engage the patients, their caregivers, neighbours, informal groups and grassroots, social and health organisations in the community. To build on the experience, there is a plan to build an ecosystem in the eastern region, with stronger and tighter collaboration with social and grassroots agencies. Extending beyond the pillars of medicine, education and research to embrace a community arm in the vision and mission of the public hospital, CGH leadership will engage the community stakeholders further to develop collective mission and vision for health in the eastern region.

With such a strong leadership, a time has come for true integration of the current fragmented services through community work. Goh has postulated that leadership involvement is of paramount importance in the creation and development of cross-sector relationships in the community.[21] A reflection of strong leadership involvement is the level of emotional connections individual leaders make with the social mission and with their counterparts in the other organisations. To create that relationship, they must agree on what it is that they need from each other to achieve it and share the benefits. Without a shared objective, meaningful cooperation is not feasible; without mutual needs, the organisations can reach it alone without cooperation even though they may share the same objectives. If they do not share the benefits, they cannot expect the commitment required for cooperation.

There must be a good fit between the hospital and its community, the facilities, missions, strategies and values. This may require continuous improvements to constantly align each organisations' priorities and resources with each other. It requires top to bottom connection at all relevant policy and operational levels. Reform of the service delivery system through incorporation of organisational strategies, including democratic management principles and empowering staff to work collaboratively with other organisations, is needed. In addition, leaders need to create a trust-sensitive environment by paying attention to the processes that facilitate good practice, communication and proactive information exchange to build inter-organisational trust. The RHS-driven community work will bring about the integration that is so needed in today's healthcare.

---

[21] Goh Soon Noi, "An exploratory study of the inter-organizational relation among health/residential long-term care services for the elderly", Submitted in Part-Fulfilment of the Requirements for the Degree of Master of Business Administration of the University of Warwick, 2000.

Chapter 5

Developing the Social Capital of Young Drug Offenders: The PST (4Ks) Model

Umardani bin Umle

Background of Drug Situation in Singapore

It takes a village to raise a child, and definitely, a more concerted effort is needed when a child is arrested for drug experimentation. In a statistical release by the Central Narcotics Bureau (CNB) in 2016, an estimated number of 300 drug abusers were below the age of 20 (see Figure 1). Though this number is relatively a small fraction of the total abusers arrested, the trends and patterns disclosed an alarming situation. It can be seen in Table 1 that there is a 130% jump of drug abusers arrested between 2005 and 2014. The number peaked in 2011 when 260 youths were arrested by the CNB before it reported a declining trend.

The government had been closely monitoring this trend, and since the 1995, an inter-ministry committee was set up, known as the Inter-Ministry Committee on Youth Crime (IMYC), and led by the then Chairman, Associate Professor Ho Peng Kee. With the setting up of such a committee, the government's resoluteness to manage the drug-taking behaviour amongst the youth was strengthened. In line with the state's narrative of

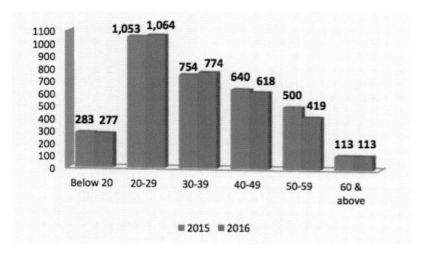

Figure 1. Total abusers by age.

Table 1. Number of youth drug abusers arrested (aged under 20).

Year	
2005	57
2006	50
2007	79
2008	89
2009	119
2010	163
2011	260
2012	190
2013	181
2014	188

Source: Central Narcotics Bureau.

Whole-of-Government (WOG) approach, various ministries were enlisted to embark on nationwide interventions to curb juvenile delinquency and youth addiction, thus recognising that such social problems are multifaceted and multidimensional. The IMYC was represented by senior officials helming various posts from the Ministry of Home Affairs, the then Ministry of Community Development, Ministry of Education, Singapore Police Force and Singapore Prison Service and other resource persons from the National Crime Prevention Council, the then Subordinate Courts and academia. The concerted efforts by the various stakeholders pronounced the need to ensure that interventions were multidisciplinary and, more importantly, had a systemic approach.

Fast-forwarding to 20 years later, the IMYC was renamed as the National Youth Guidance and Rehabilitation Committee (NYGR). One of the most significant features of the NYGR, as compared to the previous focus, is the inclusion of self-help group representatives such as MENDAKI, the Singapore Indian Development Association (SINDA) and the Chinese Development Assistance Council (CDAC). The shift to include the self-help groups is seen as a deliberate move to engage community leaders to tackle and manage the different community members within their ethnic groups. This inclusion expands the acknowledgement on the importance of working collaboratively with non-governmental organisations (NGOs), and riding on the WOG rhetoric, active participation from various community agencies such as Students Care Service, Singapore Anti-Narcotics Association (SANA), Institute of Mental Health (IMH) and many others further enhanced the collaborative approach to manage young drug abusers. This deliberate inclusion is with the recognition that community agencies have respective strengths and expertise in tackling various social issues such as addiction, delinquency and the like, thus harnessing a synergy between government bodies, statutory boards and NGOs.

The efforts that had been undertaken so far are laudable. Through promoting a collaborative approach to combat a social issue signifies the *gotong royong* or *many helping hands* approach as a narrative that Singapore has embarked since gaining independence. Through such endeavours, different members of the society are constantly engaged in a discourse on the best approach to manage youth's drug addiction and harness each member's strength to contribute according to their best capacities.

The WOG approach is not a new concept in the management of the social problems in Singapore. Vasoo noted that community development had been the buzzword since independence.[1] He argued that community development approach by the colonial administration hinged on ethnic and racialised lines to manage the various segments of the community and more importantly, acknowledging that fellow community members were more able to manage the cultural diversities and nuances. Since Singapore gained her independence, the emphasis shifted on community building as an imperative to maintain and sustain social order in the country. Vasoo further asserted that several factors interplayed to advance community development efforts and, notably, the relocation of residents and the rise of non-governmental sectors.[2] The relocation of people from a closely knitted "kampong" milieu to housing estates had the unintended effect of alienation and isolation. In the past, doors were left unguarded as a signal to welcome neighbours because familiarity with each other promoted a sense of safety. With the advent of relocation by the Housing and Development Board (HDB), the displacement of such familiar faces in different neighbourhoods increased alienation and inevitably isolation. This, as Vasoo suggested, produced a lack of neighbourliness and impersonal social identity, and more importantly, detachment to the neighbourhoods in which they live in. What was once a porous community has now turned into a gated society. The displacement brought along a host of other problems, and from a criminological point of view, solidarity amongst neighbours dwindled and with it informal social control is almost invisible. Barrett aptly described this in terms of social solidarity. A cohesive community that has a strong solidarity fortifies itself against conflicts, suspicions and mistrusts with each other.[3] Conversely, a divisive community has weak solidarity.

In the past, familiarity with each other allowed conflict negotiation to be resolved at the community level, but the modernisation of a neighbourhood relegated responsibility of management of social ills to the state. When the society becomes more complex, the rise of non-government bodies provided the state with an extended arm to manage the problems at

---

[1] S Vasoo, "Community development in Singapore: New directions and challenges", *Asian Journal of Political Science*, 9(1), 2001, pp. 4–17.
[2] *Ibid.*
[3] Gene Barrett, "Deconstructing community", *Sociologia Ruralis*, 55(2), 2015, pp. 182–204.

the community level, thus giving rise to the mushrooming of social services such as Family Service Centres (FSCs), Social Service Offices (SSOs) and others to provide the necessary assistance for the community. The ubiquitous presence of voluntary welfare organisations that have sprouted across the various neighbourhoods is very much needed to mitigate against alienation. They are seen and observed to be the ties that bind, to be the contact points between the residents and the state. Thus, community development is viewed as a critical component to mitigate against social ills such as youth delinquency, crime and addiction.

Elsewhere in the United Kingdom, community development proponents have also noted that socio-political-economic changes have an influence in shaping the community development efforts to manage a particular social problem.[4] In the example of the Scottish government, similar narratives to Singapore's many helping hands rhetoric were propagated to advance community development efforts in Scotland and it includes social inclusion, lifelong learning and active citizenship. Downie and Elrick (2000) further suggested that community development efforts should begin as early as the planning stage and involve users of such projects.[5] This strategic move can enhance active participation to manage the social issues adequately.

This chapter aims to provide a brief commentary on the national efforts to manage the drug addiction issues amongst the youth. Thereafter, this chapter highlights gaps that had not been adequately addressed and provides a mode of intervention by the SANA in the rehabilitation of young drug offenders.

Literature Review: Community Development, Desistance and Social Capital

Community development approach has been romanticised as a panacea to social ills, and different governments capitalised on this approach for their respective social problem management such as environmental and social

---

[4] Alex Downie and Deirdre Elrick, "Weaving the threads: Community development and organising around the environment — A Scottish perspective", *Community Development Journal*, 35(93), 2000, pp. 245–254.
[5] *Ibid.*

development and crime prevention.[6] Before we begin the discourse on critiquing strategies of community development in general, it is a worthy effort to define the term "community development". What is defined as "community", who are the "members of the community" and what can be considered as "community development"? It is an imperative to define what constitutes community development projects, and as Gilchrist argued, "There is a tendency amongst those working out with their own institutions to regard anything that happens 'in the community' as community development, whether or not it has any discernible developmental effect or results in significant improvements in the quality of life for community members."[7]

The term community can be defined generally as a space in which kinship is formed within a family and with the society at large. It is the building block in which stability, social order and institutions, and cultural practices are established. This translates into a social network in which members are categorised in respective roles, negotiating expectations thus framing cultural practices and social norms.[8] McAlister, in her studies on active participation in Northern Ireland, further added that the dynamism of a community is also contingent on the active participation of members during the community planning so that solutions and services are responsive to the real needs of the affected and concerned people.[9]

The term "community" may have been defined differently by the various fields but the central tenets of community seem to embody reciprocity, interaction, social networks and collective identity.[10] This then

---

[6] Mary Lane and Kaylene Henry, "Community development, crime and violence: A case study", *Community Development Journal*, 36(3), 2001, pp. 212–222; MaryAnn Brocklesby and Eleanor Fisher, "Community development in sustainable livelihood approaches — An introduction", *Community Development Journal*, 38(3), 2003, pp. 185–198.
[7] Alison Gilchrist, "Community development in the UK — Possibilities and paradoxes", *Community Development Journal*, 38(1), 2003, pp. 16–25.
[8] Gene Barrett, "Deconstructing community", pp. 182–204.
[9] Ruth McAlister, "Putting the 'Community' into community planning: Assessing community inclusion in Northern Ireland", *International Journal of Urban and Regional Research*, 34(3), 2010, pp. 533–547.
[10] Alison Gilchrist, "Community development in the UK — Possibilities and paradoxes", pp. 16–25.

features the community as an ecosystem in which different parts of the society interact, and the social exchange produces or in this case, ameliorates, a concerning social issue. Gilchrist noted that policies that centred around community development seek renewal in economic and social growth through promotion of active citizenry from all walks of life and professional bodies and inadvertently, reigniting civic engagement.[11] Thus, there is a strong signal on harnessing a collective effort, not just reliance on government, to resolve social and community issues such as the neighbourhood renewal strategy to manage crimes and high levels of unemployment. At the heart of any community development endeavour, enlisting the direct users or participants can potentially increase the sustainability of a community's resolve to a social problem. The fundamental thinking underpinning this paradigm is to engage and empower both the affected and disaffected sections of the population to reach a collective resolution against the social problem. In this sense, the manifestation of a social problem is a product of the society and a community approach is the most effective and, to say the least, the more responsible act that each member needs to uphold.

The Challenges of Desistance for Young Drug Offenders

Youth who are involved in the criminal justice system require a different paradigm for effective rehabilitation. The challenge of rehabilitation is to ensure discernment in the appropriate interventions. In the rehabilitation of young offenders in Scotland, Whyte concluded a frame of reference in understanding youth crime and rehabilitation in which youth offending relates to a broad range of vulnerabilities that the youth are exposed to in the family and social systems, cautioned a premature categorisation of at-risk youths who can run the risk of stigmatisation and highlighted that desistance from offending can either be expedited or obstructed by critical moments in early teenage years.[12] Thus, practitioners need to recognise that the criminal responsibility of the youth needs to take into considera-

---

[11] Ibid.
[12] Bill Whyte, "Effectiveness, research and youth justice", *Youth Justice*, 4(1), 2004, pp. 3–21.

tion the environmental factors and the developmental needs of the youth and that interventions not strategically positioned can further exacerbate offending behaviours.

In light of the above, the youth justice system in Scotland differs slightly from England and Wales, in the approach to punishment and rehabilitation of the youth. It is recognised that the youth crime is a manifestation of the larger problems that existed in the society at large. Given the developmental needs of the child and situations in a family system that could not be easily exited, the last resort to rehabilitate the child is actually in criminalising it. The act of criminalisation of a child's behaviour seems to connote that the child has the sole responsibility of his or her own behaviour but in actual fact, nested in a system that is not within their control due to their developmental age and needs. The criminal responsibility needs to be reconfigured. Amongst criminologists, the central argument against the risk-factor paradigm that has been integrated and weaved in most of the rehabilitation efforts globally is the obsession to identify risk factors of the offending behaviours.[13] The contention revolves around the ability of such risk assessments to predict with full confidence that young children's involvement in crime will definitely lead to adult criminal career. This is in contrast to desistance proponents that engagement in criminal acts may cease to exist due to maturation.[14]

To further advocate for a revisiting of the rehabilitation of youth offenders in Scotland, the Edinburgh Study of Youth Transitions and Crime of 4,300 young people highlighted the following significant information:

(1) Offenders have been associated with previous experience as victims of crime and adult harassment.
(2) Early identification of at-risk youth may have a reverse effect on the intended purpose. Youth who have been identified at an early stage

---

[13] Lesley McAra and Susan McVie, "Youth crime and justice: Key messages from the Edinburgh study of youth transitons and crime", *Criminology and Criminal Justice*, 10(2), 2010, pp. 179–209.

[14] Shadd Maruna, "Desistance from crime and explanatory style", *Journal of Contemporary Criminal Justice*, 20(2), 2004, pp. 184–200.

and predicted to be serious offenders may perpetuate contamination thus reinforcing the criminal thinking mindset.
(3) Arguments have been made for diversionary programmes to prevent contamination.
(4) Diversionary programmes can facilitate the desistance process.[15]

This then calls for a review on how rehabilitation efforts should be shaped and influenced by the desistance approach for a more effective solution to manage juvenile delinquency and youth crime. Future interventions need to be cognizant of the fact that young people's criminal behaviour is a product of the interactions of the social contexts such as child welfare, education and health, and social and recreational provision. Whyte posited that both human capital and social capital interventions need to be in tandem, and he acknowledged that driven by the current emphasis of risk-factor paradigm, human capital interventions such as equipping of cognitive skills take precedence over building of social capital.[16] It is insufficient as the social capital is not targeted concurrently. This is a critical issue to address sustainability of the change from within to continue to maintain the change when the young offenders interacted with the outside. Thus, programmes that did not include equal emphasis to scaffold, building social relationships with other members and minimising social participation can be an impediment for the desistance process.

Thus, viewing that youth crime is a complex product of personal, interpersonal and social factors that perpetuate the behaviour, it is imperative that a resolution towards crime management needs to involve beyond the psychological aspects and consider a more systemic approach to manage youth crime.

Building the Social Capital in the Community Development

This section will attempt to integrate the conceptual framework of community development and juxtaposing the desistance of offending

---

[15] Lesley McAra and Susan McVie, "Youth crime and justice: Key messages from the Edinburgh study of youth transitons and crime", pp. 179–209.
[16] Bill Whyte, "Effectiveness, research and youth justice", pp. 3–21.

behaviours amongst the youth. A couple of questions are in order to set the tone for practitioners in guiding their interventions. First, what are the core principles and practices of social capital that can increase the likelihood of reintegration? Second, what is the role of community in building relationships of support and control for offender reintegration?

Bazemore and Erbe suggested that current policy and practice tend to shy away from situating offenders in the context of neighbourhood organisations, thus creating a gap in which community resources can be tapped on strategically to effect a successful reintegration process.[17] One of the emerging approaches in the youth offender rehabilitation is the conscientious use of restorative practices to guide interventions.[18]

Briefly, advocates of restorative practice focus on a single but powerful concept of healing. The healing process is required in which the offence that was created leaves a trail of hurt to victims, offenders and the communities. Thus, the healing process requires seeking amendments from a strained relationship that were experienced by all parties. Bazemore and Erbe described "the importance given to social relationships in restorative processes, and in the context of reintegration, is grounded in a sense of community as interconnected networks of relationships between citizens and community groups who collectively have tools and resources that can be mobilized to promote healing and reintegration".[19]

In the context of youth's drug-taking activities, at times family members are not viewed as victims of crime in addition to the social costs that the community had to bear. Interestingly, because of the nature of the drug-taking offences, in which the harm is traditionally experienced by the offender and the society only, family members are almost invisible in

---

[17] Gordon Bazemore and Carsten Erbe, "Operationalizing the community variable in offender reintegration", *Youth Violence and Juvenile Justice*, 1(3), 2003, pp. 246–275.

[18] John Braithwaite, "Setting standards for restorative justice", *British Journal of Criminology*, 42, 2002, pp. 563–577; Gwen Robinson and Joanna Shapland, "Reducing recidivism: A task for restorative justice?", *British Journal of Criminology*, 48(3), 2007, pp. 337–358; Huang Hsiao-fen, Valerie Braithwaite, Hiroshi Tsutomi, Yoko Hosoi and John Briathwaite, "Social capital, rehabilitation, tradition: Support for restorative justice in Japan and Australia", *Asian Journal of Criminology*, 7(4), 2011, pp. 295–308.

[19] Gordon Bazemore and Carsten Erbe, "Operationalizing the community variable in offender reintegration", pp. 246–275.

the healing process despite that the punishment can be felt by the parents as well. Thus, it is imperative that restorative work includes healing the family too. Bazemore and Erbe suggested the following restorative guidelines:

(1) Restorative justice practice should not only direct the focus on emotional and material damage to individual victims but also conceptualise the various types of victims that include families and society.
(2) Restorative work should emphasise decision-making processes that involve the affected parties and ensure social capital such as families and community members make connections with the offenders and the victims to assist in the respective reintegration process.
(3) Although the psychological process of forging a new identity through a "restoring process" may occur independent of restorative processes, identifying change may also be more directly related to amends-making activity — especially when viewed in a broader, more collective context.[20]

Interventions that are based on restorative justice principles have the capacity to accelerate desistance processes by creating both new connections that build human capital in offenders and social capital in the communities where they will be reintegrated.[21] The following section will highlight an intervention that was introduced by SANA in enhancing the reintegration process of the young drug offenders.

SANA's Parent Support Talk — 4Ks

In reviewing the efforts to manage the youth drug offenders in Singapore, it is rather imperative that the practitioners synthesise evidence-based literature to optimise the rehabilitation of young abusers and reinforce the need to steer them away from future drug-taking activities. Past scholarships highlighted the need for professionals to recognise a systemic approach to reinforce the recovery of young drug offenders. This

---

[20] *Ibid.*
[21] *Ibid.*

endeavour could better utilise the confluence of theoretical frameworks from community development, desistance and social capital literature.

SANA was formed in August 1972 and its first president was the late Dr. Ee Peng Liang. He led the team in its response to the government's call to manage the drug situation back then. Through this establishment, counsellors were engaged to provide the reintegration support for ex-drug offenders. SANA has established itself in pioneering both the preventive and remedial efforts to support the recovery of drug abusers. In addition to this, SANA collaborated with CNB and the schools with the introduction of preventive drug education to students. In 2016, SANA recognised the need for a systemic and sustainable change in helping the recovery of drug abusers and piloted a programme that involves working with parents of young drug offenders.

The Parent Support Talk (PST) was conceptualised in view of the needs to engage support network in the rehabilitation of young drug offenders. It is with the recognition that it is insufficient to provide interventions with the youth only that prompted a revisit of enhancing the social capital to promote desistance. The PST was conceptualised by a team of a counsellor, a psychologist and a social worker. To complement the counselling provided for the youth, the team focused on building a conducive environment for change to ensure that the change is sustainable beyond the period of counselling. This was in line with Bazemore and Erbe's emphasis on sustainable change:

> Recognising that human capital skills that are taught in a closed setting or contained environment is not adequate, a practical strategy is also needed to allow offenders to learn social and occupational skills in settings where they are linked organically to positive adults and where the motivation for coming together with such guides or mentors is not premised primarily on the presumed need for remedial training or treatment.[22]

The outlines of the programme are as follows: The sessions are divided into two half-day sessions in which parents of the young drug abusers are invited to attend this programme. At the conceptualisation of this programme, the team recognised the importance to reduce stigmatisation amongst the

---

[22] *Ibid.*

participants, provide empowerment for the participants and seek collaboration in the support for the rehabilitation of the drug offenders.

To achieve all these, the programme focussed to make a hybrid version between a support group and educational talk. Given the time-factor as a consideration, the support group may require a longer time to achieve its objectives and attrition rate may be experienced, thus compromising on the progamme integrity. For a group to focus purely on educational talk, it may not be a conducive environment to promote a new network for the parents. Thus, recognising the need to balance between information-giving and support for the parents, the programme is split into two overarching themes that could achieve the desired outcomes.

First Session — Understanding the Drug-Taking Behaviours

In this session, the team recognises that parents are constantly in a state of ignorance about drug-taking behaviours amongst youth. The focus of this session is to create greater awareness on symptoms of drug-taking behaviours, risk factors and the consequences of drug-taking habits. Through education, parents are able to demystify the myths about drug-taking and share opinions from the experts in the field. In most cases, parents would experience shocks and anger when they first received the call from the CNB about the arrest of their children. The whole incident may trigger a rollercoaster of emotions from excessive worry, anxiety and blaming to guilt. Upon conclusion of the investigation and being referred to a community service, parents may harbour such ill feelings throughout this ordeal. Thus, the first session not only serves just mere information-giving but also implicitly helps parents in making sense of the addiction journey. To further reinforce the learning, SANA has also engaged a recovering drug addict who has volunteered to share personal life story and experience with drugs. This session provides parents with insights and the struggles from a living example.

Second Session — 4Ks

The second session is designed to divert focus from mere information-giving to providing skill sets that parents can adopt in their approach with their children. Thus, capacity-building is the underlying theme that underpins the programme structure. The team recognises that relationships at home can either be a contributing or impeding factor in youth's socialisation with negative social influences. In this session, parents are taught effective communication skills that are intended to narrow the distance between parent and child interactions and inadvertently, to promote a healthy relationship between the two parties. Briefly, parents are provided with bite-sized information that are easily retained and applied.

The 4Ks of Effective Communication

(1) **Know yourself:** Understanding the emotions and challenges in parenting.
(2) **Know the right time:** Identifying suitable moments (such as dinner time, shopping, picnics) to connect with youth.
(3) **Know what to say:** Identifying the language and reconstructing the narratives to engage youth.
(4) **Know how to say it:** Identifying the tones, the choice of words.

Throughout this session, the intended outcome is first to provide transferable skills that parents can adopt to improve the communication patterns. One of the significant features of this session is how the facilitation is structured. Parents would sit in circles instead, and employing the techniques of effective group work practice, they would discuss their past experiences and strategies in managing their youth. Inevitably, the facilitation process creates an informal support group for the caregivers in which parents learn creative ideas from other parents and the feeling that they are not alone in their struggles.

This session has highlighted a taken-for-granted assumption that parents have been working with. A general feedback from parents after the session reveals how their respective individual communication patterns may have contributed to the distance that they have created with their youth.

Learning Lessons from the PST (4Ks)

In the implementation of this programme, there were several valuable lessons that were acquired to improve the rehabilitation of young drug offenders more effectively. More importantly, targeting the healing process appropriately at different vantage points can help to improve the social capital of the young offenders.

Social Exchange and Social Support

It is important to recognise that to have a family member, particularly a youth, arrested for drug-taking behaviour is something that no one is feeling proud of. The shaming not only comes when an arrest is effected but a sense of blaming also hurts the family system. Thus, creating a safe and non-intrusive environment for similarly situated individuals can accelerate the healing process. Participants are supported through a sequence of sessions that first focus on making sense of the situation, hearing from a life example and thereafter learning new skills from one another. This experience in itself creates a sense of community amongst the parents and became a new source of support for each other whilst supporting their children's recovery from drugs. In this healing process, parents do not feel alone in their struggles as they have observed similar experiences by others. This segment also enables parents to increase their human capital, and at the same time, creates a new network with others in their support to help the youth desist from drug-taking behaviours.

Making Amendments and Reparation to Community

The team is cautious of holding a session that would include the youth themselves. Thus, through creative persuasion, ex-drug offenders volunteer to share life stories as part of the programme. From the ex-abuser's point of view, the healing takes on a different level and through sharing, it further reinforces his narrative to re-script one's identity to a redemptive one. Despite the fact that there is no pre-existing kinship between the parents and the ex-abuser, the disclosure is empowering for both the parents and the recovering addict.

Professional Roles and Identity

Bazemore and Erbe identified the role of the professional as an advocator and broker to enable the offender to develop prosocial relationships between offenders, adults and the community groups.[23] Through distributing equal emphasis of developing both the human and social capital, practitioners can further set the stage for the community and the various systems to scaffold in the rehabilitation of the offenders.

Conclusion

Youth crime is inevitable in all the jurisdictions, and constant review of the latest developments in the scholarship can help promote evidence-informed practices. Community development has evolved over time, and generally, the central tenets focus extensively on multi-collaboration and active participation from members of various sectors. Specific to youth-centric endeavours, practitioners and researchers need to be in cognizance to expand from risk-focused practices to include systems-centric practices in order to optimise rehabilitation of the youth.

---

[23] *Ibid.*

Chapter 6

Using Narrative Practices in Community Development for Children and Families Living in Vulnerable Estates

Mohamed Fareez and Elisha Paul Teo

Introduction

This chapter discusses the incorporation of ideas from *narrative therapy* into community work with children and their families who live in rental and transitional housing estates in Singapore.[1] Practice examples from local Singaporean social work organisations such as Ang Mo Kio Family Service Centre (AMKFSC) Community Services are also discussed.

The Narrative Perspective

Narrative therapy is a framework of working with people, groups and communities, with theoretical foundations influenced by Foucault's ideas in social constructionism (1988), narrative psychologies and social

---

[1] David Epston and Michael White, *Narrative Means to Therapeutic Ends* (New York: W.W. Norton, 1990).

anthropology.[2] Narrative practices are also influenced by feminist and social justice theories. Narrative community workers seek to move away from the expert position of the helper and choose instead to privilege the knowledge and skills of the community. A narrative approach accords privilege to the stories of these persons and communities and seeks to establish a respectful and non-blaming approach to social work practice. It views problems as separate from people and assumes that people are not passive respondents to the problems they face, but instead have the skills, competencies and knowledge to deal with them. This was clearly stated by White in the following terms: "Our participation in community assignments is based on the understanding that we cannot know, ahead of our engagement with them, what might be the knowledges of life and skills of living appropriate to achieving the goals of the people of these communities".[3]

Key Principles in Narrative Community Work

Defining Experiences and Problems within Local Knowledge

Drawn from Article 1 of the draft charter of storytelling rights, this principle seeks to move away from global, Western and oftentimes pathological definitions of people's experience.[4] Instead, narrative practice privileges local knowledge and understandings of the experiences of people and communities. As Baretto and Grandesso stated, "when people's local knowledge is devalued, this leads to an interiorization of misery: misery becomes an internal experience ... the situation is made worse if they seek assistance from people who only value academic knowledge and do not value local knowledge".[5]

---

[2] Tina Besley, "Foucauldian influences in narrative therapy: An approach for schools", *Journal of Educational Enquiry*, 2(92), 2001, pp. 72–93.

[3] Michael White, "Narrative practice and community assignments", *The International Journal of Narrative Therapy and Community Work*, 2, 2003, pp. 17–55.

[4] David Denborough, "Healing and justice together: (Draft) charter of storytelling rights", Presentation at the Launch of Re-experiencing the Rojak: Narrative Therapy and Community Work in Singapore, 3 October 2017.

[5] Adalberto Barreto and Marilene Grandesso, "Community therapy: A participatory response to psychic misery", *The International Journal of Narrative Therapy and Community Work*, 4, 2010, p. 34.

Community development hence would involve consulting communities about the struggles that they are going through, through their lived experiences and through definitions that are derived from their own work. Community workers suspect any judgment and analysis of the problem, but instead privilege members' understandings of the struggles they are going through.

A Profound Belief in Community Members' Understandings and Abilities

This is clearly articulated by Russel, who argued, "One of the foundations in narrative work with communities involve holding a profound belief in people's understanding of their life and abilities in managing their lives".[6] This is based on the premise that community workers subscribe to the mindset that as professionals we do not have the answers to the issues raised. The answers are often found through social workers making conversations with the community members to uncover their solutions to address those issues. Social workers hold the opinion that it is the community members who possess the "insiders' knowledge" to their issues and have the ability to overcome such problems.

The Person Is Not the Problem, the Problem Is the Problem

This is a key philosophy of narrative therapy, which seeks to ensure that problems are not located within people.[7] Community workers take care to identify experience-near themes and understandings of problems following consultations of local knowledge. However, at the same time, community workers have to work ethically to ensure that problems are not defined as located within people. For example, in a group for single mothers, a participant had discussed about a "violent husband", a theme which was built upon by other participants to be about "violent men". Social workers would then need to negotiate descriptions which are reductionist. In this case, social workers had instead talked about the "culture of violence" that men are susceptible to, due to patriarchal structures that men are socialised into.

---

[6] S. Russell, Personal Communications, 18 September 2008.
[7] David Epston and Michael White, *Narrative Means to Therapeutic Ends*.

Doubly Listening for Skills, Values and Knowledge

Narrative practices start from the assumption that communities are able to respond to the hardships and struggles they face.[8] These can be "practical know-how" in responding to difficulties and going about life. They may be embedded in tradition, spirituality and culture. It is the role of the community worker then to identify rich stories of these values, skills and knowledge, through the tracing of their histories, and details of how they are used to overcome struggles. A key skill of practitioners would be that of "doubly listening" where the practitioner listens not only to the accounts of hardship and suffering but also to actions that are made by individuals and communities to respond to these struggles.[9] In this way, community workers do not discount the struggles faced by these communities; rather, they are concerned about how the socio-political factors in the environment are also contributing to these struggles. They are interested to listen to the absent but implicit: stories and experiences that may describe shared values, hopes and dreams of the community.

This would then allow personal agency to develop within members of the community. As was stated by White, "Community Consultations that are guided by this principle of doubly listening are unlikely to contribute to circumstances in which team members become overwhelmed, or in which team members might initiate actions from outside of the context of the partnership that we have with other team members ... It is highly likely that these conversations will also be sustaining of the purposes of the team members, and will be reinforcing of the sort of team member action that is in accord with the terms of these contracts".[10]

The "Gift of Giving": Enabling Contribution

This is a philosophy of practice adopted by the Mt. Elgon Self-Help Community Project when finding ways to involve children in meeting their

---

[8] Michael White, *Narrative Practice and Community Assignments*, pp. 17–55.
[9] *Ibid.*
[10] *Ibid.*

needs in non-blaming, respectful and empowering ways.[11] For example, in community projects where a child is involved in a poultry project to raise their own chicks, they would be encouraged to also give one of their chickens to another child who is planning to be involved in the project. Enabling members of the community to be able to initiate contribution allows children and their families to be seen as "active contributors" and "agents of change", as opposed to being passive and "static" recipients of welfare services. When members of the community are able to contribute, there are opportunities for people to see themselves as valued members of society.[12]

Linking Lives through Shared Purposes

One of the tenets of narrative therapy is the intentionality of practitioners to link people together. This could be as simple as bringing together two people from the same community so that they could share how to struggle with a particular kind of problem. A key element in any narrative community project is this linking of lives through shared purposes.[13] Social workers intentionally create platforms for people to share stories of their struggles and how they acquire knowledge gained from those struggles.

Definitional Ceremonies: Platforms for Communities to Perform Preferred Identities

The concept of Definitional Ceremonies was developed from the work of social anthropologist Barbara Myerhoff, who had studied a Jewish community who were living their aging years in Venice, California.[14] Through

---

[11] Caleb Wakhungu, "The gift of giving: Empowering vulnerable children, families and communities in rural Uganda", *The International Journal of Narrative Therapy and Community Work*, 1, 2014, pp. 30–32.

[12] *Ibid.*

[13] Jill Freedman and Gene Combs, "Narrative ideas for consulting with communities and organizations: Ripples from the gatherings", *Family Process*, 48, 2009, pp. 347–362; Jill Freedman and Gene Combs, *Narrative Therapy: The Social Construction of Preferred Realities* (New York: Norton, 1996).

[14] Barbara Myerhoff, "Life not death in Venice: Its second life", in Victor Witter Turner and Edward M. Bruner (eds.), *The Anthropology of Experience* (Urbana: University of Illinois Press, 1986).

their activities in the Israel Levin Senior Centre, these people were able to relive aspects of their histories and traditions that were important to them. The definitional ceremony is about creating a social arena where the participant's preferred stories could be richly described to an audience. Hence, intentional platforms are created to allow participants to enact their preferred stories to an audience who would be able to resonate with their preferred selves.[15] Children from families affected by vulnerabilities represent members who may have "spoiled identities".[16] Under normal circumstances, they would not have natural opportunities to appear before others to display and share their preferred interpretations of their lives. Children in poverty who are affected by low educational functioning, thus, have limited opportunities to have their skills, knowledge and abilities celebrated by an audience.

Denborough discussed how community workers can identify existing definitional ceremonies to draw people together, drawing on "folk culture" to identify rituals that are already being practiced in the communities that community workers are working with.[17] In Singapore, the community worker may tap on block parties and community events in partnership with the local community centres and residents' committees (RCs), as potential platforms for definitional ceremonies. Singaporean definitional ceremonies could also take place in barbeque sessions by the beach, during religious activities such as the reciting of the "tahlil" in Islamic practices of offering prayers in respect for the deceased, house warming celebrations, end of the Primary School Leaving Examination (PSLE), during festivals and many more.

Linking Stories and Initiatives

This is a practice developed from the idea of definitional ceremonies, where community workers seek audiences to witness stories of preferred identities. This form of community engagement involves the exchange of

---

[15] Michael White, *Maps of Narrative Practice* (New York: W.W. Norton & Co., 2007).
[16] Erving Goffman, *Stigma: Notes on the Management of Spoiled Identity* (Englewood Cliffs, New Jersey: Prentice-Hall, 1963), pp. 1–147.
[17] David Denborough, *Collective Narrative Practice: Responding to Individuals, Groups, and Communities Who Have Experienced Trauma* (Adelaide, South Australia: Dulwich Centre Publications, 2008).

stories and messages across two or more communities at a time.[18] Documents and publications may be created to facilitate this process. The key characteristics according to Denborough *et al.* are as follows:

(a) Documents use the exact words and phrases of the people being interviewed.
(b) Documents are double storied — as much as they richly describe the struggles that the community is going through, they also describe the strategies and steps that the community is taking to respond to the struggles.
(c) Documents are structured along significant themes that are common across the community's experience, e.g. the experience of shame after divorce. Community members' response are also arranged in themes, e.g. the skills of "heck care" to respond to "shame".
(d) Documents include the values, skills and knowledge of the community, their histories and how the community has managed to hold on to them.[19]

Rich details of responses to hardships allow social workers to pursue the narrative that people are not passive recipients of trauma.[20] These collective documents could then be shared across communities to obtain responses via the outsider witness structure where questions were structured around the following:

(a) Expressions — What words caught your attention or captured your imagination?
(b) Image — What image do you have about what the community values?

---

[18] David Denborough, Carolyn Koolmatrie, Djapirri Mununggirritj, Djuwalpi Marika, Wayne Dhurrkay and Margaret Yunupingu, "Linking stories and initiatives: A narrative approach to working with the skills and knowledge of communities", *The International Journal of Narrative Therapy and Community Work*, 2, 2006, p. 21.
[19] *Ibid.*
[20] Angel Yuen, "Less pain, more gain: Explorations of responses versus effects when working with the consequences of trauma", *Explorations: An E-Journal of Narrative Practice*, 1, 2009, pp. 6–16.

(c) Resonance — Why do you connect with the images and expressions? What parts of your own life connect with the stories being shared?

(d) Transport — What are you inspired do to on account of hearing the story? How did the stories move you? What steps would you take in your own lives on account of having heard this story?[21]

Sharing these stories across communities and groups of people allows for previously isolated communities and persons to feel a sense of connection and be acknowledged for the skills, knowledge and values that were practised in response to the hardships being faced in their lives. According to Denborough *et al.*, this practice may bring comfort to communities, especially since their responses to hardship are being respected and treasured by others, creating the experience of personal agency.[22] In the same vein, Baretto and Grandesso argued, "… we're interested in creating a sense of solidarity, a sense of compassion, a sense of 'my problem is not the worst', or 'I am not the only one with this problem'. We're also trying to create a public space in which there's no conformist agenda, there's no one way to live life … this renewed sense of personal agency, a sense of being able to be a protagonist in one's own life, is what we hope participants will carry …"[23]

Narrative Ideas in the Singaporean Context

In this chapter, we will discuss a few Singaporean community projects that have been utilising ideas of Narrative Community Work. They include the League of Parents and Small People against Pocket Kering, The Mothers M-Powered Programme, the Achieving Kids (AK) Programme as well as

---

[21] Michael White, *Maps of Narrative Practice*.
[22] David Denborough, Carolyn Koolmatrie, Djapirri Muṅunggirritj, Djuwalpi Marika, Wayne Dhurrkay and Margaret Yunupingu, "Linking stories and initiatives: A narrative approach to working with the skills and knowledge of communities", p. 21.
[23] Adalberto Barreto and Marilene Grandesso, "Community therapy: A participatory response to psychic misery", p. 41.

the Friends 'N' Neighbours (FnN) project.[24] A key feature in these local projects is also how group work modalities were utilized to consult different communities affected by struggles and hardships. This then informed community development, where different groups were empowered to address these issues at the community level, whilst social workers were also mobilised to source and provide resources, create conversations and partnerships and advocate for community change in collaboration with the collective voice of the community.

The League of Parents and Small People against Pocket Kering

This community project, led by Elizabeth Quek was formed in 2013 in collaboration with families, living in the Bukit Merah and Chinatown estates in Singapore, who were receiving financial assistance and supported by a family service centre (FSC).[25] These were essentially families who were affected by poverty, which was named "Pocket Kering", after consultations by Quek with her co-workers, based on their experiences of working with the community. "Pocket Kering" (Kering literally translated from Malay into "dry") represented an experience near description of the poverty that these families were susceptible to. It was further conceptualised and externalised into the "Pocket Kering" Monster, allowing a safe space to engage with children about the effects of poverty in their lives, especially since it was reported that their parents struggled when talking about such issues with their children.

The project sought to recruit children and uncover their local knowledge and skills in responding to poverty or towards the "Pocket

---

[24] Elizabeth Quek, "Presenting the League of Parents and Small People against Pocket Kering: Debuting the skills and knowledges of those who experience financial difficulties", *The International Journal of Narrative Therapy and Community Work*, 2017, pp. 26–40; Mohamed Fareez, Anny Rodjito and Isaac Teo Lai Huat, "The Mothers M-Powered Programme — Community based group work with mothers living in the interim rental housing estates", 2017, https://www.ssi.sg/SSI/media/SSI-Media-Library/learning-n-development/NarrativeTherapyebook.pdf.

[25] Elizabeth Quek, "Presenting the League of Parents and Small People against Pocket Kering: Debuting the skills and knowledges of those who experience financial difficulties", pp. 26–40.

Kering" Monster, through the metaphor of seeking superheroes to unite against the "Pocket Kering" Monster.

The Mothers M-Powered Project

The Mothers M-Powered Project, conducted by social workers from AMKFSC Community Services, is an example of how group work overlaps with community work, emphasising that personal issues can be situated within the political space.[26] Social workers were initially expected to respond to the spate of child abuse cases in the interim rental housing (IRH) community, by conducting a psychoeducational parenting programme. An invitation instead was made during outreach for mothers who were interested to share not only the struggles they faced in parenting their children amidst unstable housing arrangements but also to identify the skills and knowledge they used to respond to the various challenges associated with transitional housing. The group of five mothers were initially consulted through six group work sessions, using narrative ideas of remembering (identifying key persons or family members in their lives who supported them in overcoming their struggles), and the tree of life methodology, where participants drew a tree with parts representing aspects of their preferred identities such as their skills (trunk), hopes and dreams (branches) and important people in their lives (leaves).[27]

This consultation enabled the group to identify their problems based on their own words and identify the skills they used based on their own words. For example, mothers identified "focusing on education" and "teaching children right values" as key practices that they adhered to despite the multiple stressors they faced in having to move homes multiple times. Their struggles and responses were categorised into themes and collated into a booklet, which would serve to represent their collective voice of the group.

---

[26] Mohamed Fareez, Anny Rodjito and Isaac Teo Lai, "The Mothers M-Powered Programme — Community based group work with mothers living in the interim rental housing estates".

[27] David Denborough and Ncazelo Ncube-Milo, *The Tree of Life Manual* (Adelaide, South Australia: Dulwich Centre, 2008).

Using the principle of the "gift of giving", the group was further encouraged to share their collective voices in the context of a definitional ceremony.[28] For the first run of the programme, participants set up a booth during a Community Day event conducted for residents living in the IRH estate. They would then distribute these collective documents to other mothers and residents living in the community, opening further conversations within the community itself about tapping on local skills and knowledge in parenting children in the face of unstable housing and multiple family stressors. This simple activity of showcasing their hidden talents presents a definitional ceremony platform where the mothers can live their preferred identities in ways that are acknowledging. Outsider witness responses were also collated through comments by the public upon reading the documents, to further thicken these preferred alternative storylines.

Subsequent runs of the Mothers M-Powered Programme have also used a structured outsider witness process, where members of the community, family members and social workers performed the role of an audience to listen to participants sharing excerpts of their collective document. Audience members would then respond using the outsider witness format of expressions, images, resonance and transport.[29]

The Achieving Kids Programme

AK is a community development programme run by AMKFSC Community Services targeted at children aged 7–12 years living in the rental blocks in Ang Mo Kio. Under the programme, staff and volunteers would play the role of *friendly visitors*, inspired by the work of pioneer social worker Mary Richmond. Friendly visitors would engage families with children to identify the issues faced by families living in low-income neighbourhoods. More importantly, they would also identify assets and skills of these children and their families that could be harnessed to address community issues. Academic coaching, children's interest groups and

---

[28] Caleb Wakhungu, "The gift of giving: Empowering vulnerable children, families and communities in rural Uganda", pp. 30–32.
[29] Michael White, *Maps of Narrative Practice*.

character-building programmes are also conducted using community spaces at three different areas.

Influenced by narrative ideas, social workers would frequently consult the children on the struggles that they are experiencing in the community and collaborate with the children to discuss on the ways these issues could be tackled using the skills and abilities that they were already practising. For example, when requested by the neighbouring community centre to run workshops to teach children ways of coping with examination stress, instead of coming in from an expert position, social workers conducted a two-session group work with children who were invited to share the skills that they were already using to cope with stress. Social workers then planned together with these children on the activities in the booth (which played the function of the definitional ceremony), where they could share their skills with other children in the community.

Again, drawing from the group work as part of community work modality, when concerns were raised about children participating in acts of vandalism in the community, as opposed to just working with the identified children who had been participating in vandalism, social workers invited all students in the programme to participate in a group to address "vandalism" in the community. Together the children could discuss the effects of seeing unsightly graffiti in the community and could collaborate to mobilise ways to improve the environment, through cleaning and campaigning projects.

The use of collective documents had also allowed "ephemeral" conversations to be thickened through the written word and be expanded into the realm of community development.[30] For example, the Girls' Talk was a group work intervention process that came about through the engagement and consultation of young women aged 9–14 living in the IRH community. These women were consulted about the dominant discourses of women, and their stories and strategies of how they overcame limiting discourses were thickened and documented. As the young women had questions about puberty and relationships, social workers introduced professional and academic knowledge tentatively, whilst also listening for

---

[30] David Denborough, *Collective Narrative Practice: Responding to Individuals, Groups, and Communities Who Have Experienced Trauma.*

their own ways of coping with the changes in their lives. For example, practical advice from the young women were obtained on managing "cramps when they get too painful".

Young children in vulnerable communities have limited opportunities to have their views and self-worth acknowledged; hence, creating platforms where they are able to practice the "gift of giving" contributes to an increased sense of self-worth and the experience that their life stories are being acknowledged and valued. Within a community development perspective, tapping on "insider knowledge" would definitely be experience-near ways of engaging communities to have conversations about their struggles, and the strategies that have worked in overcoming them, as opposed to using purely professional and academic knowledge.[31]

Collective practices using music have also been used to link and share the stories of children living in the IRH estates who experienced multiple transitions. Songs can be used as a medium for children to celebrate their strengths and connect different communities together. The following Truck Song had also been instrumental towards informing funders and partners of the multiple stressors' children in transition housing face, in efforts to garner resources and volunteer support for these children.

The Truck Song

(Voices of children living in the Interim Rental Housing Estate)

Packing up belongings, load it up the truck
Friends and neighbours, I'll miss you, time to say goodbye
At least we still have Facebook, I'll see you there online

Found ourselves in a strange new place
With room so small I can barely rest my head
Not sure I'll like this place, but who knows what awaits

Know new friends, some became our very best
Oh what fun, playing our games together
A Life, RC (Resident's Committee) and outings are memories we can't forget

---

[31] David Epston and Michael White, *Narrative Means to Therapeutic Ends*.

The truck will move again
To where I could not say
Memories good or bad
I'll bring along with me

The truck will move again
To where I could not say
No matter where it brings me
I'll find a way to my dream

— Music arranged by Melvin Yeo

Friends 'N' Neighbours (FnN) Programme

The FnN is a community development programme that seeks to identify and empower residents living in low-income communities in the Ang Mo Kio estate in Singapore. Residents living in low-income communities may perceive their community as lacking in community resources and dependent on professional services to obtain the resources their communities require. Social workers engage in conversations with residents to identify individual skills and link the community assets to strengthen social networks in the community. Participants typically live in one- or two-room rental flats in Ang Mo Kio. Social workers identify a committee of 12 persons, who would meet monthly to identify issues in their communities that they hope to address. The community would plan and run programmes and events for other residents in the community (enabling contribution) in the hope of increasing social capital. These events facilitate cross-generational interactions.

When the programme first started in 2015 at one of the rental blocks in Ang Mo Kio, residents were extensively consulted through focus group discussions about the struggles and hopes they had for the community. Social workers conducted the focus group discussions initially with the intention of engaging vulnerable older adults who were living alone and isolated in the community who might require additional socio-emotional and practical support. What instead became interesting for social workers was when these residents (who had been identified to be "vulnerable") shared their hopes to meaningfully engage children who were often seen loitering at the void decks till late night. Residents also shared about the dearth of socio-recreational events for the community, which they felt was important to families who have limited financial capacities to organise or participate in such events.

The focus group discussions led to social workers and residents partnering to organise a Community Day in the form of a "Block Party". This "Block Party" allowed residents to uncover "hidden assets" found in their community such as individuals who could sing and perform, produce art pieces and more. This discovery led to residents feeling more confident that they could work on the issues and challenges faced by the community.

From the "Block Party", residents were identified and volunteered to form the 12-person committee to meet regularly. The FnN committee planned festivities along the lines of the four local ethnic festivals commonly celebrated in Singapore (namely the Chinese Lunar New Year, Hari Raya, Deepavali and Christmas). Residents felt that their neighbours might not be open to seek professional services even if they might have a need. By using the festive celebrations, residents felt that their neighbours were more likely to be drawn out of their homes to participate in such events. By attending such events, neighbours would get better acquainted with one another and the professionals in the community, such as the RCs and the FSC. Residents were also able to witness for themselves how the level of "neighbourliness" increased after each event, as neighbours would greet one another in the lifts and at the void decks. Small conversations were created and the residents felt that their neighbours subsequently made efforts to know one another, which helped to lower the rate of isolation experienced by certain individuals or families.

When planning the festive celebrations, social workers consulted and discussed with the residents throughout the planning to execution stage on what and how they would envision the festive celebrations to look like. Residents were active in designing the flyers, door-knocking to their neighbours to pass flyers, inviting their neighbours for the celebration, asking if neighbours were keen to contribute food items to share with the community and organising the list of programmes for the actual day of celebration, which became crucial components in building self-agency and increased their self-esteem and sense of belonging to their community.

Community Days

Community Days are definitional ceremony platforms that are organised to support the many programmes conducted by AMKFSC Community Services. Twice yearly, social workers would collaborate with committees and residents living in either the IRH estates or the subsidised public rental estates to organise a "Block Party". This would usually be held either in the nearby multipurpose hall or under the void deck to celebrate and showcase the skills and assets of the community.

The Community Day platform is based on the narrative principles of celebrating local knowledge, creating platforms for participants to showcase and thicken their preferred stories. This practice is a shift from past practices of organising family day events for clients. In the past, these family day events were intensively planned and run by professionals and volunteers to facilitate family bonding and incorporate preventive and developmental strategies in parenting and addressing family conflict. A key feature of the family day event is that it was professional-led, and hence tended to privilege academic knowledge instead of local ones. Children and their families would then be passive recipients of these interventions, further replicating the one-down positions that were evident in the other aspects of their lives.

The Community Day modality is instead conceptualised as an alternative to the family day events. It is in fact a platform to showcase counter stories of skills, knowledge and values, with the chief aim of celebrating the strengths of the community as opposed to attempting to educate residents of community concerns from a top-down perspective. This platform would assist in the development of a definitional ceremony that allows for further retellings and creations of rich descriptions of the lives, values and skills of the residents living in the area. Community Days are stakeholder-conceptualised and stakeholder-led, with social workers playing facilitative and supportive roles.[32] The Community Day platform also sees residents staying in the IRH estates coming together to co-create remembrance of families' rich histories. These families used to stay at different parts of Singapore and brought with them vast

---

[32] Barbara Myerhoff, "Life not death in Venice: Its second life".

collections of memories from their past. Residents would take ownership to setup stalls and organise performances.

Conclusion

This chapter has presented the key principles of narrative practice that could apply in working and engaging communities in Singapore and has also identified community initiatives that have been conducted using these principles. There is further need for research and evaluation on the effects of components of narrative practices on social capital and individual well-being. One known qualitative study on narrative community work evaluated the Back from the Edge project by the Dulwich Centre and Relationships Australia, which was a community project that sought to respond to the high rates of suicide and suicide attempts by the young people of the Gunyangara and Yirrkala communities in Australia.[33] The report found that the project had contributed to an increase in self-esteem and confidence of members in the community. There had been a reduction in the number of suicides in the communities, although the report stated that it would be difficult to measure whether this change could be solely attributed to the outcomes of the project alone.

Narrative community development seeks to move from the dominant discourse of seeing communities affected by difficulties as being passive recipients of support from formal institutions and social workers. It seeks to instead leverage on community skills and knowledge, through an intentional process of consultation, in order to collaboratively find solutions to challenges faced in communities. The case examples show that these ideas do not have to be adopted in the purest sense, but can also be adapted to complement existing models of community work. It is important that these ideas are contextualised into Singapore's unique multicultural environment, considering rituals and definitional ceremonies that are relevant to Singaporean cultures.

---

[33] Sonja Berthold, "Back from the edge: Project evaluation. Relationships Australia Northern Territory", 2006, Retrieved from http://www.dulwichcentre.com.au/back-from-the-edge-evaluation.pdf, 7 July 2015.

Chapter 7

Community Development with Lifelong Learners in Action for Change

Samuel Beng Teck Ng and Belinda Choh Hiang Tan

I heard about YAH! on the radio and was intrigued with the idea of going back to school — to learn again at the ripe age of 64! Being Chinese-educated and with a primary school education, I was apprehensive. After talking to my daughter, I took the courage and enrolled into the YAH! Lifelong Learning Programme.

YAH! has a lively and energetic learning spirit. I love how it brings elderly together to explore, discuss and talk about the issue of daily life and it inspired me to continue to learn even after my graduation.

When I was diagnosed with third-stage nose cancer more than 5 years ago, during my chemotherapy and radiotherapy treatments, the doctor would ask me to think of a happy place or happy memories, I thought about my children and grandchildren, I thought about YAH! and my love for learning; and that was what got me through.

I would really like to thank YAH! for giving me a late start at 64. YAH! has transformed my life and given me new meaning to my half time.

Rose, 75, Batch 1 of YAH! Certificate in Lifelong Learning.

YAH! Enables Seniors through Education and Community Development

Opportunities in the Silver Tsunami Years

With a sizeable number of seniors in Marine Parade, Montfort Care's founder and Chief Executive, Samuel Ng, saw opportunities in harnessing the potential of seniors to build a stronger community. There was a strong belief that through education, seniors will be able to achieve their personal outcomes and more importantly, that of the community. Piloted in the Marine Parade Family Service Centre in July 2005, Young-at-Heart (YAH!) was the first lifelong learning programme for seniors in Singapore. This pilot subsequently evolved into the YAH Community College. Today, the Marine Parade Family Service Centre and YAH! are programmes under Montfort Care.[1] As a social worker, Samuel firmly believed that developing individual seniors to serve the community was the cornerstone for the inception of YAH!. His primary desire was to promote social change, build relationships, empower people and improve their psychoemotional well-being.

YAH! Certificate in Lifelong Learning

Popularly known to the Mandarin-speaking seniors as 快乐学堂, the YAH! name exudes the elements of fun and happiness in learning to the seniors, boosting their lives and enhancing their sense of achievements in the golden years. Its lively school song also befits the learning atmosphere.

The YAH! Certificate in Lifelong Learning then consisted of a 100-learning hour curriculum. Conducted over three-and-a-half months, the curriculum consisted of three 30-hour modules: a core module on applied gerontology, two elective modules on self-enrichment courses and

---

[1] Montfort Care is a network of programmes committed to improving the lives of individuals, families and the community facing transitional challenges. Today, Montfort Care focuses on two key areas — family and eldercare. Under its family services, it operates the @27 FSC in Telok Blangah, Marine Parade FSC and Kreta Ayer Family Services. In its recent eldercare service expansion, GoodLife! has gone beyond Marine Terrace. It now reaches out to seniors in Bedok, Kaki Bukit, Kreta Ayer, Marine Drive and Telok Blangah. In the next two years, it will also expand to other new sites. YAH! and Big Love are programmes under its specialised services.

a community project work. The remaining 10 hours were for homework and self-reflection.

The applied gerontology aims to equip the seniors with knowledge on the biological, psychological and social aspects of ageing. Topics covered included dispelling myths of ageing, physiological changes, importance of family and community support, fears of death and dying, caregivers' challenges and communications skills. These modules, coupled with the group work approach by social workers, strive to make our seniors better prepared for their ageing process, transformation, as well as new developmental phases in their third age.

The programme has evolved over the years, with several name changes, from Certificate in Lifelong Learning to Certificate in Life Transformation. Today, it is known as the Happy 50.

Supporting Women in Their Third Age

Realising that older women who stay alone are particularly susceptible to poverty and social isolation, YAH! reaches out to the "heartlanders", especially women, 50 years and above. This early wisdom on the needs of women with limited education was gleaned from Samuel's own mother who despite having little education, persevered and brought up the family singlehandedly and continues to have the zeal to pursue her dream in learning.

Today, YAH! has over 2,500 alumni members. Majority of them are housewives with limited or lower educational qualifications who aspire to fulfil their "mortar board" dream. Over 85% of them are female, with 78% of them in the 60–70 age group. Of the members, 70% are married, while 30% are single, widowed or divorced. Over 85% of them have an educational level at the secondary level and below.

Desired Outcome

The desired outcome of the pilot was to use lifelong learning as a means to perform the following:

- Impart knowledge and skills to the seniors to enable them to cope with their transitions and to lead a self-reliant and active lifestyle.

- Support seniors in their psychosocial needs during their life transitions.
- Inculcate the value of productive ageing through self-care and transform them into leaders.
- Change the social perception of ageing through advocacy, public education and seniors' active participation in the community.

The YAH! Model

The core beliefs of YAH! are "Transformation", "Empowerment" and "Contribution" as shown in the YAH! Learning Pathway. When seniors are enrolled into YAH!, they would experience the mindset change guided by the spirit of YAH!. As they participate in its peer learning activities, they experience cognitive, emotional and social change leading to the next level of transformation.

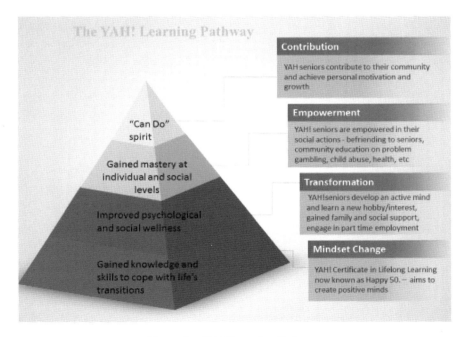

Figure 1. YAH Learning Pathway.

Source: YAH Community College. ScholarBank@NUS Repository.

Based on Jack Mezirow's theory of adult learning grounded in cognitive and developmental psychology, the YAH! Learning Pathway also adopted the experiential and peer-based learning approach where our senior learners go through a process of making sense to their own experiences through reflection, critical reflection and critical self-reflection.[2] The seniors were also supported by the YAH! social/case workers and their peers in their psychoemotional development, enabling them to draw out their positive strength.

In the Later-Life Learning — A Case of YAH! Community College by written by Mr. Ee, who stated that participants shared on their expanded social networks as well as having more confidence due to the supportive environment in YAH!.[3] Seniors also shared that the inspiring curriculum, conductive learning environment and supportive learning have resulted in an increase in their self-efficacy. This newfound confidence and changed perspective in their dilemmas also enabled them to let go of the negativities in their lives.

At the next level, for learning to be purposeful, the seniors were empowered to make sense of their new achievements and were challenged to lead and work together and to deepen their engagements with themselves and the community. Under the YAH! Senior Leadership Programme, the seniors became Community Mission Ambassadors for health and problem gambling prevention. As ambassadors, they were responsible for the planning, communications and delivery of the community service and activities, enabling them to learn and practise working in teams as well as empowering them to demonstrate their unlimited potential. According to Dirkx (1998), "Through connectedness with community transformative learning leads paradoxically to a deeper sense of one's self as a person".[4] A survey conducted in 2006 by YAH! on the effects of lifelong learning on older adults' personal well-being showed that 92.1% of the 237 YAH! seniors reported an increase in their happiness and self-esteem level.

---

[2] See Colin Calleja, "Jack Mezirow's conceptualisation of adult transformative learning — A review", *Journal of Adult and Continuing Education*, 20(1), 2014, pp. 119–134.
[3] Ee Cheang Ching, *Later-Life Learning: A Case Study of YAH! Community College* (Singapore: ScholarBank@NUS Repository, 2010).
[4] John M. Dirkx, "Transformative learning theory in the practice of adult education: An overview", *PAACE Journal of Lifelong Learning*, 7, 1998, p. 10.

YAH! Eco-Learning Model

Following the successful pilot, YAH! introduced its YAH! Eco-learning Service Model to illustrate the continuous learning journey of our YAH! seniors through social learning, social action and social movement.

To support the seniors in social learning, YAH! further expanded its learning repertoire to overseas learning journeys. In 2007, the seniors visited the Beijing Tsing Hua University, followed by the Nanjing Jin-Ling University of Third Age and the Shanghai University of Third Age, just to name a few. The YAH! seniors also participated in learning forums such as the Singapore–China Lifelong Learning Forum and the Ageing Industry Summit Forum. In addition, a series of Certificates in

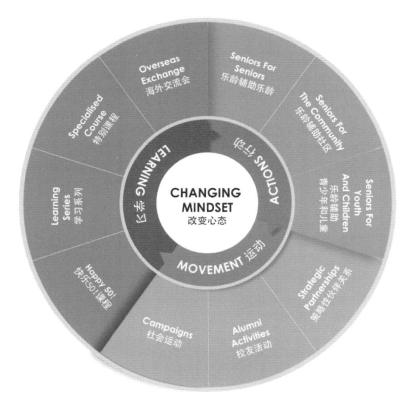

Figure 2.   The YAH! Eco-learning Service Model.

Source: YAH Community College. ScholarBank@NUS Repository.

Community Education and Learning Hives were also introduced. Initiated "by the seniors, for the seniors", the Learning Hives tapped on the knowledge, experience and skills of YAH! seniors to organise and provide the learning programmes in accordance to their needs. This peer-based learning was effective in enabling and empowering the seniors.

From Beneficiaries to Contributors in Social Action

While the Learning Pathway continues to lay the foundation in its eco-learning model, the social action programme, Happy Club, offered social actions programmes serving seniors, children, families and the community. This is to entice the seniors who have benefitted from YAH! to contribute to the areas that resonate with their interest, transforming them from beneficiaries to contributors in their society.

Under its "Seniors for Seniors" programme, the YAH! seniors brought life and friendships to other seniors and caregivers in the community through befriending, learning and social activities. Notably, senior beneficiaries whom they served in the community drew inspiration from the YAH! seniors, in changing their perception on age and challenged some of their notions that "old is good for nothing". Seniors who participated in the "Seniors for Children" programme conducted reading programmes to children at the Bishan Public Library as well as reached out to children in the schools on child abuse public education. This intergenerational interaction provided both generations to learn about one another and establish better understanding.

Under the "Seniors for Community" programme, YAH! has been a key player in the Problem Gambling Prevention Ambassadors Campaign since 2009. With the construction of two casinos in Singapore, the YAH! seniors also wanted to do their bit to prevent problem gambling. Since then, the YAH! seniors continue to conduct public education on problem gambling and responsible gambling at the betting outlets and the Singapore Turf Club. Through the partnership with the National Council of Problem Gambling (NCPG), outreach was further extended to patrons at private clubs and foreign workers in recent years. With the public speaking and skit performance training from YAH!, seniors were further empowered to develop and evolve the scripts for their responsible gambling skits. In 2016, they were invited to perform at the Responsible Gambling Awareness Week as well as conducted outreach programmes at community events and launches such as Jiak Pah Buay TV series promotional roadshow in Toa Payoh.

From Learners to Advocators in Social Movement

Having benefitted from the YAH! social learning and action programmes, the seniors were engaged in its social movements to change societal perception on ageing and the old, from a liability to an asset. In the "I Love Seniors" movement in 2013, over 100 YAH! seniors and Republic Polytechnic youths joined hands to stage a flash mob to change the public perception on ageing. In their sporting outfits, the YAH! seniors together with the youth performed a lively dance which surprised the crowd at the mall. Among the dancers was retired businessman Cheong Choon Hee, who celebrated his 76th birthday that day. A 2009 YAH! graduate, Choon Hee is an active YAH! social action participant. He said, "I want to celebrate my birthday in a special way this year. I want my family to participate in the flash mob dance with me as I want to show that ageing isn't about losing yourself or slowing down."

Annually, YAH! seniors also participated in the International Older Persons movement to raise awareness about issues affecting seniors. They also partnered schools in social movements. With the increasing spate of seniors involved in road accidents, YAH! seniors together with the Bishan Park Secondary School students promoted "Care for Seniors on the Road" in 2016 at Raffles Place and other public places. Over the decade, YAH! has continuously reviewed and evolved its service model to ensure its relevancy and meeting the aspirations of the seniors. From its social learning, the YAH! seniors moved on to partake in social actions and movement, growing from the "me to the we" in its eco-learning model. The YAH! programme is now offered at Bedok, Marine Parade, Kreta Ayer, Toa Payoh and Telok Blangah.

Impact of YAH! Programme

Guek Kew's learning journey in YAH! and transformation is an exemplary showcase of the impact of the YAH! programme.

> *Guek Kew given away at a very tender age, had only a primary 5 education. She had a tough childhood as she was often bullied by her siblings.*

Her life did not improve after her marriage as her family was constantly plagued with spirits, bad familial relationships and she had to single-handedly support the family and her two sons.

Guek Kew first read about YAH! in the Lianhe Waobao in 2005 and wanted to enroll in the YAH! Programme. She wanted to participate in the social action programmes as deep down Guek Kew has always wanted to help those who are worse-off than her. However, as a very shy and introverted person, Guek Kew did not have the courage to venture out. She finally decided to join YAH! eight years later.

With good peer support, encouraging learning culture as well as the psychosocial support from the YAH! social workers, Guek Kew became more confident and started to open up by the fourth lesson. She shared, "I am a totally different person today. I am thankful for YAH! as it has helped me to discover my potentials and given me knowledge and skills to work on my family relationships. I used to be so aloof and unhappy but look at me now, I am chatty and happy!

This is the best time of my life as I am a lot happier now. While I still worked part time, I set aside some days for community service. The more I do, the more happiness I received. I want to do more!" she added.

Guek Kew is a regular face in our social action programmes, ranging from befriending, caregivers' support to organizing learning and social activities for others in the community. Together with a group of her YAH! friends, they teach Mandarin to the children in Batam with the aim that the skills can enable them to find work in the retail and travel industry in future. Her participation in YAH! local and overseas community service has not only broadened her perspective in life but also fulfilled her dreams of serving others.

Tan Guek Kew, 64, Batch 28 YAH! Certificate in Life Transformation in 2013.

Concept and Theoretical Frameworks Adopted by YAH!

Third Age and Active Ageing

The YAH! Service model was guided by development theories such as Erikson's theory of psychosocial development, Maslow's hierarchy of needs and Laslett's four phases of the human lifespan.[5] Laslett introduced the first age as the early socialisation where a person learnt skills and knowledge and was dependent on others, the second age is when a person focuses on career development and financial independence, the third age is when a person has fulfilled most of his responsibilities, in family rearing and career, and has the autonomy to enrich one's intellectual as well as spiritual capacities. In the fourth age, frailty sets in and one is highly dependent on others for support.[6]

YAH! subscribes to the belief that the third age is full of opportunities for the older persons and 50 is the beginning of the golden age. It is the time where most of our seniors would have fulfilled most of their responsibilities, and still be mobile, healthy and possess the ability to continue to learn and make a difference in the community, contributing to a purposeful half time.

According to the World Health Organization (WHO), "Active Ageing is the process of optimising opportunities for health, participation and security in order to enhance quality of life as people age".[7] The quality of life is a "broad ranging concept, incorporating in a complex way a person's physical health, psychological state, level of independence, social relationships, personal beliefs and relationship to salient features in the environment".[8]

Transformative Learning to a Positive Quality of Life

Numerous literatures from Educational Gerontologists on later life learning can attest that education is the key to active ageing. WHO also acknowledges that education and learning are key to participation and allow older persons to have a positive quality of life. Apart from providing knowledge and skills, the YAH! programme was also anchored on transformative learning with a focus on the psychosocial development of seniors. Its end goal, being the pursuit of enabling seniors' participation in community development, makes the YAH! programme uniquely different.

---

[5] For example, see Abraham H. Maslow, *Motivation and Personality* (New York: Harper, 1954); Erik H. Erikson, *Childhood and Society* (New York: W. W. Norton & Co., 1950).
[6] Peter Laslett, *A Fresh Map of Life: The Emergence of the Third Age* (London: Weidenfeld and Nicolson, 1989).
[7] World Health Organisation (WHO), *Active Ageing: A Policy Framework* (Geneva: WHO, 2002).
[8] *Ibid*, p. 13.

Transformative learning is an individual and social process. It not only enhances the independence of the individual but also empowers them to make social changes collectively.[9] Using group work and peer-based learning approaches in its learning process, the therapeutic group work facilitated by YAH! social workers and alumni members enabled the seniors to share their inner thoughts in a safe environment. Aptly put, "the essence of group work is that a group is more than the sum of its individual members".[10] The peer-based learning has resulted in higher receptivity to learning.

As noted by Toseland (1995), "Peer learning enables and facilitates a greater volume of engaged activities and successful practice, leading to consolidation, fluency, and automaticity of core skills".[11] This is evident as we witnessed other seniors being motivated to participate when they saw the YAH! seniors of their age and those who were older leading and organising activities, giving a new narrative on what ageing means.

Community Development Leading to Greater Empowerment

Literature has also shown that community volunteering can transform the older persons into more active participants in community development.[12] Embracing the approach where community development is one of the core components, the YAH! social action programme provides opportunities to foster active participation among seniors and allows contributions to the community to achieve self-actualisation.[13] Through education, training

---

[9] Edward W. Taylor, "Analysing research on transformative learning theory", in Jack Mezirow (ed), *Learning as Transformation: Critical Perspectives on a Theory in Progress* (Jossey-Bass, San Francisco, 2000), pp. 285–228; Mark C. Tennant, *Psychology and Adult Learning*, 2nd edn. (New York: Routledge, 1997).

[10] Ronald W. Toseland, *Group Work with Elderly and Family Caregivers*, 4th edn. (Springer Publishing Company, 1995).

[11] Keith J. Topping, "Trends in peer learning", *Educational Psychology*, 25(6), 2005, pp. 631–645.

[12] Jeremy Rifkin, *The End of Work: The Decline of the Global Labour Force and the Dawn of the Post-Market Era* (New York: G.P. Putnum, 1995); Lester M. Salamon, "The rise of the nonprofit sector", *Foreign Affairs,* 73 (4), 1994, pp. 109–22.

[13] Community development is defined as an employment of community structures to address social needs and empower groups of people. See Phillip Mendes, "Teaching community development to social work students: A critical reflections", *Community Development Journal*, 2008, p. 3.

and empowerment of our senior leaders, YAH! social workers facilitated the organising of self-help, shaping their actions and environment. As facilitators, the professional work involved the creation of interest groups and supporting them to engage with institutions such as NCPG, Singapore Turf Club and other stakeholders.[14] While they worked in teams, the sharing of mutual experiences and concerns amongst the seniors helped them to realise that they are not alone and aided them in their transitions and coping with issues. The group dynamic, together with the YAH! spirit, provided an identity to the group.

Adopting the Empowerment Theory and Activity Theory, YAH! enabled the seniors to think positively about their abilities and they also gained mastery over promoting problem gambling and seniors' issues.[15] Empowerment also included the notion of self-efficacy, that is, perceptions of competence, personal control and positive self-image.[16] Being empowered, the YAH! seniors soared to greater heights as they led and worked in teams to contribute to the community. In problem gambling, their efforts were recognized when the Ministry of Social and Family Development accorded them the "Friends of MSF" award for their efforts in problem gambling prevention in 2015. The YAH! seniors who participated in Happy Clubs were also able to achieve positive ageing (through maintaining roles and relationships) and experienced positive relationship between social activity and life satisfaction in old age.

The "Can-Do" Spirit of YAH!

"What I have learnt from YAH! is the 'Can-Do' spirit. To learn when I can, and to give when I can," said Kong Wee, a father of two, and a retired technician.

---

[14] Saul D. Alinsky, *Rules for Radicals* (New York: Random House, 1971).

[15] Marc A. Zimmerman, "Empowerment theory: Psychological, organizational, and community levels of analysis", in Julian Rappoport and Edward Seidman (eds.), *Handbook of Community Psychology* (New York: Springer Science and Business Media LLC, 2000), pp. 43–64; Yrjö Engeström, Reijo Miettinen and Raija-Leena Punamäki, *Perspectives on Activity Theory* (Cambridge University Press, 1999).

[16] Marc A. Zimmerman, "Empowerment theory: Psychological, organizational, and community levels of analysis", pp. 43–64.

Kong Wee came to Singapore to work in his teens and eventually started his family here. Having gone through hardship in his younger days, he believes in seizing every opportunity that comes his way; especially now that he has fulfilled his family rearing responsibilities.

"YAH! is like a rock wall as it has supported me to go further and higher than I could on my own. I love learning for the same reason; it allows me to rise and made me a better person and open new doors for me to create new experiences." said Kong Wee. Till today, Kong Wee remains an active Happy Club member and has been serving as a Problem Gambling Prevention Ambassador as well as a GoodLife![17] Angel ambassador, befriending vulnerable and stay-alone seniors in Marine Parade.

Chow Kong Wee, 77, Batch 2 of the YAH! Certificate in Lifelong Learning.

His participation in a rock-climbing challenge was documented in a 2009–2010 television series — "I can do it" which also featured 23 other YAH! Alumni.

We have witnessed the growth and development of our YAH! seniors — the more they give, the more they learn and grow personally over the years. While many seniors volunteer to occupy time, YAH! seniors' positivity towards life and in particular age, grew as they volunteer more. They also became more confident and happier as they gained greater awareness of their own abilities and capabilities. Happy people are open to the world and are more self-confident.[18]

Annually, YAH! seniors have outreached to over 30,000 members of public through their social action in promoting problem gambling prevention, conducting outreach activities to stay-alone seniors and caregivers as well as conducting reading programmes in the libraries. Today, many of them also participate in arts, environment, culture, other social services agencies as well as overseas community services, contributing to the greater good.

---

[17] GoodLife! is a wellness programme for seniors under Montfort Care. Its Angel Ambassador programme is a befriending programme to support seniors in the community.

[18] Alex Zautra, *Emotions, Stress, and Health* (New York: Oxford University Press, 2003).

Relevance of Theories and Concept in the 20th Century

According to theory of the third age by Laslett, old age further comprises the third and fourth ages.[19] His theory implied that elders who are healthy are thus third agers, whereas others who are frail are the fourth agers. Laslett also depicted the older person in third age as one who exercises fuller autonomy in self-fulfilment as he assumed that all were middle-class, educated, financially sound and with equal access to information and resources. While this framework is useful for service planning, it is too simplistic. In reality, human development is multifaceted and more complex.

What Laslett did not take into account is the impact of the external environment, such as public policies and economic conditions. In this current world economy faced with increasing cost of living, limited job opportunities and rapid digital advancement, older persons will struggle with financial independence.

Financial Security

The extension of the mandatory retirement age has delayed the older persons' entry into their third age. With the increasing cost of living, the changing notion of retirement and the extension of mandatory retirement age have resulted in more seniors retiring from their full-time work, switching to part-time work so as to continue to earn an income. The SkillsFuture initiative to support skills training for seniors in recent years has also encouraged seniors to upgrade and earn an income through freelance/part-time work.

Education

Notably, the ability to access information between the haves and have-nots has resulted in a growing number of marginalised older persons. In 2015, in support of SG50, many lifelong training

---

[19] Peter Laslett, *A Fresh Map of Life: The Emergence of the Third Age*; Peter Laslett, "The emergence of the third age", *Ageing and Society*, 7, 1991, pp. 133–160.

programmes for seniors were offered for free or heavily subsidised. Seniors who were more educated, have larger social networks and have better access to information were better able to enrol in the programmes. Seniors who have little education and limited social network, on the other hand, were not as aware of the offerings available, and hence were deprived. Even if they were keen to enrol to lifelong learning opportunities, they may not have the time as they need to work to maintain their livelihood.

Gender Biasness

Even in the third age, women are often not given equal treatment as their male counterparts. For men, retirement marked an important life stage where their status changes from being a worker to a non-worker. While transitions into retirement is easier for the working women as they are likely to continue with their family care role, it often impedes their participation. At YAH! where most of our seniors are housewives, they are often not available in the evenings as they need to prepare dinner or look after their grandchildren. We also often received feedback from women that they have no time for YAH! activities as they still need to take care of their family or grandchildren or a sick one in their family. According to Bernard and Meade (1993), "Throughout the life course it appears that women remain more preoccupied with what are termed as 'essential activities': domestic work, shopping, cooking, washing and so on".[20]

Another aspect that has been overlooked is the theory of generation and the power of shared experience across the life course as well as how cultural diversity among older persons have influence on their participation.[21] For seniors who have a university education, they will find the YAH! programme less desirable.

---

[20] Miriam Bernard and Kathy Meade, "Third Age lifestyle for older women?" in Miriam Bernard and Kathy Meade (eds.), *Women Come of Age* (London: Edward Arnold, 1993), p. 157.
[21] Karl Mannheim, "The problem of generations", in Paul Kecskemeti (ed.), *Essays on the Sociology of Knowledge: Collected Works*, Vol. 5 (New York: Routledge, 1952), pp. 276–322.

Montfort Care — YAH!'s Experiences

Community Partnerships for Better Outcomes

Building partnerships is imperative in community work as the pooling of resources and expertise cannot be undermined. It took Montfort Care — YAH! more than a decade to achieve its success in working with multiple stakeholders in Marine Parade and in problem gambling prevention. This did not come easy, as the relationship, mutual respect and understanding of one another's roles and capabilities took trust and time to build.

One of the key successes for Montfort Care is due to its leaders, social and community workers who were not only good facilitators but also the clarity of the programme outcomes which enabled both internal and external stakeholders to align to a common goal of building a stronger community. However, this is not always the case as we have also experienced situations where the good intentions of our seniors were rejected. Disappointed, the seniors then uprooted themselves and moved to serve another community.

Currently, there are multiple stakeholders, from the Residents' Committees (RCs), the Pioneer Generation ambassadors, self-help groups, religious groups, Community Network of Seniors and Voluntary Welfare Organisations (VWOs) groups to corporates and schools, operating in the same community space. While this is a welcome sign as they have good intentions, the community they serve can get confused if there is no coordination and possibly resulting in wastage of resources. In Marine Parade, WeCare@Marine Parade has provided the critical linkage and resources for stakeholders to work together.

Mendes argues that "spraying-on" community as a solution to social problems provides no guarantee of progress outcomes.[22] This is due to the different funding and key performance indicators which each stakeholder is committed to. Access to power, resources and information, as well as having the right connections to the authority have also made community development work more complex.

---

[22] Phillip Mendes, "Classic texts no. 5", *Community Development Journal*, 41(2), 2006, pp. 246–248.

While empowerment of communities is important, the overly zealous energy may create confusion to not only the stakeholders but also the beneficiaries. The recent launch of Community Network of Seniors in several constituencies aims to support ageing-in-place; however, we would need to keep in mind that communities comprise individuals and they have the capability to fend for its disadvantaged.[23] Through community development, we can strengthen the capability building of the people as active citizens through community groups and networks, and the capabilities of institutions and agencies to work in dialogue with citizens to shape and determine changes in their communities.[24] The community workers, together with stakeholders, can influence action planning. As noted by Carpenter and Purcell (2012), "The ideal would be when the communities, which are both empowered and empowering for themselves and to those around them are in the strongest position to influence, while agencies, which are both empowered and empowering for themselves and those around them are open and receptive to community influence, and individuals who are both empowered and empowering to themselves and those around them are active community and public life".[25]

With all the stakeholders jointly aligning the desired outcome with their funding, we believe it will provide better accountability to the efforts and outcome.

Working with Seniors

In working with seniors, the relationship- and rapport-building are key to gaining buy-in and participation. While we continue to face a shortage of social workers, it is even harder to attract social workers who are passionate in eldercare work, particularly in active ageing. Most social workers and case workers prefer to work with children and families who are down and out and the active seniors are not deemed to be needy.

---

[23] Siau Ming En, "Community support services for the elderly to cover more areas", *Today*, 23 July 2017.
[24] Mick Carpenter and Rod Purcell, *The Lisbon Papers: Transforming Leadership and Empowering Communities* (Oxford: University Oxford Press, 2012), p. 19.
[25] *Ibid*, p. 50.

The added challenge for this preventive work is the ability to find workers who are skilful, mature and patient in addressing the needs of the seniors as well as having the ability to manage their personal agenda, competitions and conflicts.

While time was needed to build strong relationship and partnership, we also recognised that there are challenges in retaining senior volunteers as well as staff. While there are solutions to sustaining the seniors' interest, maintaining their health status is beyond us. Over the years, we see the attrition of our senior volunteers not only due to their interest but also the decline of their health status. To overcome this, continuous recruitment and training efforts must be ongoing and sustained.

Importance of Good Outcomes and Community Support

Branding and good programme outcomes are also key to the continuity of the programme. One of the most powerful referrals is through the word-of-mouth of our seniors who have benefitted from our programmes. At roadshows and open house, they would enthusiastically interest other seniors to join YAH!. The good support of mass media as well as the continuous recognition of our efforts from the community and stakeholders have also enabled YAH! to sustain its efforts over the past decade.

Other Learnings

In community development approach, we also need to be mindful of patriarchal themes in leadership, where it is traditionally viewed as men's role and women are not treated equally. We need to consider adopting feminist community development approaches to citizenship, power and influence. As 85% of YAH! seniors are female, we have also learnt to work around their schedule in our planning. From social learning to social action programmes, we work with our stakeholders and partners to ensure that the activities are held in the weekday mornings so that they can partake in community service. Additionally, we also need to be sensitive to the multicultural diversity amongst our seniors to minimise conflict.

It is also important to document the service planning and development of programmes for learning, service review and improvement. For YAH!, we were fortunate and we applaud the efforts of National University of Singapore (NUS) Master in Social Sciences student, Cheang Ching Ee, who completed a study on later-life learning — A Case Study of YAH! Community College in 2010, for her Masters' programme. However, we could have done more research to document the long-term impact on the development of our seniors.

Recommendations for the Changing Landscape

Co-Creating Solutions

YAH! is the pioneer in lifelong learning as well as a trendsetter in leading the seniors in community development. We are happy that lifelong learning is one of the national agendas now. The inclusion of the programmes offered by the institutes of learning under the National Silver Academy (NSA) for which YAH! is one of the providers now offers more than 10,000 learning places across its 500 courses.[26] With lifelong learning under the ambit of the Ministry of Education and the increased access to learning in post-secondary education institutes (PSEI), we also hope to see more sharing of resources such as school premises and IT labs with non-profit organisations to conduct lifelong learning programmes for seniors as well as in community development work. This will enhance the accessibility to learning for seniors with mobility issues. The incorporation of understanding ageing in the school curriculum and learning journeys to eldercare organisations is another area that can be expanded as the inter-generational engagement would stand the young in good stead.

With the increasingly ageing population, it is imperative for the community to co-create solutions. To encourage asset-based community work, there is a need to review the current silo funding model by the Ministries to drive the behaviour on the ground. While the People's

---

[26]The NSA is a network of post-secondary education institutes (PSEI) — comprising the Institute of Technical Education (ITE), polytechnics, universities, arts institutions and other community-based organisations offering a wide range of learning opportunities to seniors. https://www.moh.gov.sg/content/moh_web/home/pressRoom/pressRoomItemRelease/2016/-learn-for-fun--learn-for-life--at-the-national-silver-academy.html.

Association has the mandate as the key player in community development, partnerships with other stakeholders cannot be ignored due to the different strengths each partner brings to the community. This huge potential human capital to co-create solutions should be tapped. According to findings from the National Survey of Senior Citizens, among those aged 55 and above, only 6% reported volunteering in the last 12 months.[27] Hopefully, the launch of the S$40 million Silver Volunteer Fund by the Ministry of Health and Tote Board will drive more participation and innovation to senior volunteerism.[28]

Research Development

Currently, there is limited local research conducted to document and analyse the active ageing efforts and the social impact generated. While we were fortunate that one of NUS Masters programme study conducted a study based on YAH! seniors, we would not have the dedicated resources and expertise to conduct such a study on our own. Such studies are key to understanding the engagement of seniors in community development through social learning and action. Embarking on research into active ageing will enable us to also better prepare for the generations after the baby-boomers generation. With the current funding criteria for NSA programmes being based mainly on the number of learning places taken up, there is little or no incentives for any VWOs to pursue in research.

YAH! has been successful for the past decade. However, the journey was not an easy one. Today, we are seeing changing profiles of seniors who are more educated, better informed, healthier, digitally savvy, wealthier and have more avenues for active ageing participation than the generations before. The changing profile of seniors, coupled with rapid policy changes due to SkillsFuture, makes it timely for us to pause, take

---

[27] https://www.duke-nus.edu.sg/care/wp-content/uploads/National-Survey-of-Senior-Citizens-2011.pdf.

[28] The Silver Volunteer Fund was launched on 4 September 2015 to encourage more seniors to share their time, expertise and energy to various social causes. The Fund will support the training of seniors as volunteers, and build capabilities in various community organisations to recruit, develop and support seniors as volunteers. https://www.pc.org.sg/Silver-Volunteer-Fund.

stock and review our current service model to ensure its relevancy for the next lap. Notably, it is not fair to measure our programme success by the number of learning places as that is the current funding model. For YAH!, we are not a training provider but an agent for community change. We hope that the catchy and chirpy YAH! song will continue to remain in the hearts of the many YAH! seniors but change would be the only constant in time ahead.

Mike was a manager in a shipping company and he practically "live to work" — totally no leisure life, no hobby as well as no friends outside work. When he retired at the age of 61, it was a bed of roses for him for the first six months, but soon, he became bored.

Like many other YAH! learners, he came across a feature on YAH! Transformation Programme and decided to enroll into the programme. He was curious about YAH's idea of ageing with a purpose and its advocate that life after retirement could continue to be meaningful and exciting.

Mike said, "It was like a mysterious door opening up endless possibilities for me and I was intrigued." In class, seniors are encouraged to share their interests and dreams. It inspired Mike to explore things that he never had neither the time nor the luxury to do so before. He took up singing, acting and public speaking and found himself drawn to performing. Since then, there was no turning back for Mike as he used his skills in performing arts to educate other seniors about issues of problem gambling.

In my younger days, I was too consumed with work to know what volunteerism was all about. If you were to ask me when I was 50, whether I would ever imagine myself performing at this age, I would have given you a resounding 'No'. YAH! empowered me to explore my interests and led me to do things that I love and I have discovered the new me!" said Mike.

Mike concluded: "The old me used to live for work; now I live for my passions".

Mike Goh, 70, Batch 21 of the YAH! Certificate
in Lifelong Learning Course in 2011.

Chapter 8

Youth Participation in Community Development: Challenges and Potential

Helen Keng Ling Sim and Irene Y. H. Ng

Introduction

Youths are a part of the community they reside in. They have talents and skills that adults may not possess and can be active contributors. Aided by technology such as portable smart devices (e.g. smart phones and tablets), youths today are better placed to respond quickly to community needs compared to youths a generation ago. As digital natives, they are comfortable with various social media and are familiar with social cause advocacy on such platforms. For example, they could have liked or retweet tweets related to various social causes on Twitter, hashtagged and posted pictures on community activities on Instagram or started a Facebook page to raise funds for a community project. The connectivity between people via technology today has made it more convenient for youths to rally support for community efforts.

This chapter highlights some of the main challenges youths face in their bid to play their part for their community. It defines youth involvement in community development and looks at how adults as community gatekeepers could facilitate or hinder their involvement. The challenges of youth–adult partnerships (Y–AP) are also discussed. The chapter ends with some suggestions on how youth participation in community development can be encouraged.

Youth Participation in Community Development

Loosely defined, youth participation refers to the engagement of youths in society. A Report by the United Nations General Assembly defined youth participation as including "four components: economic participation, relating to work and development; political participation, relating to decision-making processes and distribution of power; social participation, relating to community involvement and the peer group; and cultural participation, relating to the arts, music, cultural values and expression".[1]

Such definitions that simply describe "what is", however, do not give the essence of when one can say that youths have participated. If youths are allocated tickets to a cultural event, is that participation? If youths volunteer as ushers in a community event, is that participation? By the above general definition, yes. However, advocates of youth participation will be uncomfortable to count these examples as youth participation.

Thus, there appears to be *what youth participation is* in a general sense, and also *what youth participation is that benefits* youths and the society. The latter is what this chapter is interested in, and for this, participation literature points to the importance of involving stakeholders (in this case youths) in decision-making in things that matter to their lives.

More specifically, given the chapter's focus on youth participation in community development, Vasoo's definition of community development is helpful: "Community Development is defined as efforts either jointly or on their own of Government, corporate sector community organisations, not for profit groups or voluntary welfare organisations (VWOs) to promote community betterment and community problem solving by

---

[1] United Nations General Assembly, *Implementation of the World Programme of Action for Youth to the Year 2000 and Beyond. Report of the Secretary General*, 2001, p. 2, Retrieved from http://www.youthpolicy.org/basics/2001_WPAY_Implementation_Report.pdf.

involving people based on mutual help or self-help and planned changes. The outcome is community ownership in promoting community well-being".[2]

Extending from Vasoo's definition, youth participation in community development can be defined as "youths' efforts, either on their own or jointly with Government, corporate sector community organisations, not for profit groups or VWOs, to promote community betterment and community problem solving by involving people based on mutual help or self-help and planned changes. The outcome is community and youth ownership in promoting community well-being."

This definition suggests the following outcomes when youths have participated in community development:

(1) youths take initiative, responsibility and ownership;
(2) the efforts by the youths involve working with the target community (this could be youths themselves) and often also involve working with other stakeholders in the community;
(3) the community is bettered or a community problem is solved as a result of the youth participation.

Why Youth Participation?

Youth participation is a way to bring about social justice, youth development and community building.[3] The United Nations Convention on the Rights of the Child (CRC), one of the most widely ratified human rights agreements in the world, clearly states youths' right to express themselves freely, have a say in decisions affecting them and have their views taken seriously according to their age and maturity.[4] When youths are accorded

---

[2] S Vasoo, "Promoting participation among the young in community development efforts: Issues and challenges", Unpublished Report, n.d.

[3] Shepherd Zeldin, Steven Eric Krauss, Jessica Collura, Micaela Lucchesi and Abdul Hadi Sulaiman, "Conceptualizing and measuring youth-adult partnership in community programs: A cross national study", *American Journal of Community Psychology*, 54(3–4), 2014, pp. 337–347.

[4] UNICEF, *The Convention on the Rights of the Child*, n.d., Retrieved from https://www.unicef.org/rightsite/433_468.htm.

decision-making rights in community development, their voices can be heard and they have a say in shaping their community as active citizens.

Youth participation has also been adopted as a strategy for youth development to hone attitudes and skills which are better "caught" than "taught" in a classroom setting.[5] It has been associated with the development of an array of attitudes and skills such as interpersonal skills, multicultural orientations and the formation of identity in youths.[6] In other words, youth participation is promoted for their own good; adults and institutions do it in order to develop them.

However, beyond participation being a right of youths and with the purpose to develop them, youth participation actually benefits both the community and the society.[7] Around the world there are countless examples of youth action benefiting communities. One of the most well-known examples is the founding of Facebook by Mark Zuckerberg and his friends while they were still students. Another example is Kiara Nirghin, a school girl in Johannesburg, who invented a superabsorbent polymer using orange peel and avocado skins to store water, to deal with the drought issues in her community. She won the Google Science Fair's Community Impact Award for Middle East and Africa in 2016.

In Singapore, several examples of youth-initiated and youth-led community betterment programmes were analysed by Ng.[8] These included a "by youths for youths" organisation that develops youths through sports, service learning and character-building activities; an anti-binge drinking campaign that became a movement and a social enterprise providing life skills training to youths.

---

[5] Ho Kong Chong, Hasliza Ahmad, Helen Sim and Ho Zhi Wei, "Social participation in a new Singapore", in Victor R. Savage (ed.), *Singapore @ 50: Reflections and Observations* (Singapore: The National University of Singapore, 2015), pp. 38–46.

[6] *Ibid*; Heather L. Ramey, Linda Rose-Krasnor and Heather L. Lawford, "Youth-adult partnerships and youth identity style", *Journal of Youth and Adolescence*, 46(2), 2017, pp. 442–453.

[7] Irene Y. H. Ng, "Youth participation: Can we trust youths to lead the community?", in *Youth Scope* (Singapore: National Youth Council, 2012); Barry Checkoway, *Adult as Allies*, n.d., Retrieved from http://www.wkkf.org/knowledgecenter/resources/2001/12/Adults-As-Allies.aspx.

[8] Irene Y. H. Ng, "Youth participation: Can we trust youths to lead the community?".

To realise the full benefits of youth participation, both youths and adults need to overcome their limiting views of youths' ability to contribute and have the courage to let youths take the reins. Extending from Checkoway, Ng discussed three following "isms" that act as barriers to youth participation:

- Adultism assumes that "adults are better than young people, and are entitled to act upon young people in many ways without their agreement".[9] Examples include youth programmes planned by adults without inputs from youths themselves.
- Tokenism pays lip service to youth participation, involving youths in token ways that show surface participation, but where youths are not really involved. Involving youths as ushers, and not in the organising or giving of inputs into a community event, is an example of token participation.
- Elitism occurs when only outstanding youths are engaged, for example, the top-performing students in the school or most prominent youths in a group.

Tokenism and elitism stem from adultist attitudes. When adults do not trust youths, they assign roles only to one or two exceptional youths and engage them in token ways. Unfortunately, such attitudes lead to limited participation, limited youth development and limited benefits. The tremendous energy, creativity and ideas that youths can offer are not harnessed. Furthermore, meaningful and inclusive youth participation will be mindful to engage groups that tend to be excluded, e.g. females, at-risk youths, quiet youths, youths from minority races, youths with disability and low-income youths.

Making Youth Participation Happen: Youth–Adult Partnerships in Community Development

While overcoming the "isms" of youth participation, it also does not mean that youths should be left alone to their own devices. Afterall,

---

[9] Barry Checkoway, *Adult as Allies.*

they may lack certain experience and resources that adults possess. Adult mentorship and facilitation can complement their youthful creativity and energy. In community development, adults are typically community gatekeepers; they hold decision-making powers and resources (e.g. access to spaces, funds and networks) in the community. To illustrate in more concrete terms, a youth-led development programme for children living in a rental block with ready participants may find it hard to operate if they are denied access to community spaces by the adult gatekeepers.

The concept of Y–AP has been promoted by scholars as effective for youth and community development,[10] and offered a working definition of Y–AP: "Youth–adult partnership is the practice of: (a) multiple youth and multiple adults deliberating and acting together, (b) in a collective [democratic] fashion, (c) over a sustained period of time, (d) through shared work, (e) intended to promote social justice, strengthen an organisation and/or affirmatively address a community issue." From the definition, it is clear that Y–AP is not about having youths do everything of importance with little or no guidance from adults. It is also not about adults "getting out of the way" or "giving up power" so that youths could "gain power" as that construes power as a "zero-sum equation".[11]

Zeldin *et al.* presented the concept and measure of Y–AP in two dimensions — "youth voice in decision-making" (YVDM) and "supportive adult relationship" (SAR).[12] In Y–AP, youths are empowered to take on

---

[10] Linda Camino, "Youth–adult partnerships: Entering new territory in community work and research", *Applied Developmental Science*, 4(1), 2000, pp. 11–20; Shepherd Zeldin, Brian D. Christens and Jane L. Powers, "The psychology and practice of youth-adult partnership: Bridging generations for youth development and community change", *American Journal of Community Psychology*, 51(3–4), 2013, pp. 385–397; Shepherd Zeldin, Steven Eric Krauss, Jessica Collura, Micaela Lucchesi and Abdul Hadi Sulaiman, "Conceptualizing and measuring youth-adult partnership in community programs: A cross national study", pp. 337–347.

[11] Linda Camino, "Pitfalls and promising practices of youth-adult partnerships: An evaluator's reflections", *Journal of Community Psychology*, 33(1), 2005, pp. 75–85.

[12] Shepherd Zeldin, Steven Eric Krauss, Jessica Collura, Micaela Lucchesi and Abdul Hadi Sulaiman, "Conceptualizing and measuring youth-adult partnership in community programs: A cross national study", pp. 337–347.

meaningful decision-making roles in a reciprocal youth–adult relationship and are connected to community networks.[13] Y–AP therefore includes youths and adults in joint decision-making from vision casting, planning and evaluation.[14] Focusing solely on youths in Y–AP is therefore misplaced as Y–AP considers the development of youths *and* adults[15] (with an element of co-learning).[16] Zeldin and colleagues summarised the core elements of Y–AP to be authentic decision-making, natural mentors, reciprocal activity and community connectedness.[17]

While scholars agree that Y–AP is central to quality youth participation, Y–AP has not been as widely adopted as desired as it is not easy to implement the concept well in practice.[18] The practice of Y–AP requires individuals to carve out time, disrupt routines and set aside the traditional roles of youths and adults to become co-learners.[19]

In addition, "community arenas are governed not only by individuals, but also by a number of overt and subtle established structures and relationships of power".[20] Community institutions have their processes and rules, and individuals are subjected to them. Y–AP is practised in the context of these processes and rules which could facilitate or hinder. An example of how an organisational rule affected Y–AP will be shared in a later section.

---

[13] Heather L. Ramey, Linda Rose-Krasnor and Heather L. Lawford, "Youth-adult partnerships and youth identity style", pp. 442–453.

[14] Shepherd Zeldin, Steven Eric Krauss, Jessica Collura, Micaela Lucchesi and Abdul Hadi Sulaiman, "Conceptualizing and measuring youth-adult partnership in community programs: A cross national study", pp. 337–347.

[15] Linda Camino, "Pitfalls and promising practices of youth-adult partnerships: An evaluator's reflections", pp. 75–85.

[16] Shepherd Zeldin, Brian D. Christens and Jane L. Powers, "The psychology and practice of youth-adult partnership: Bridging generations for youth development and community change", pp. 385–397.

[17] *Ibid.*

[18] Shepherd Zeldin, Steven Eric Krauss, Jessica Collura, Micaela Lucchesi and Abdul Hadi Sulaiman, "Conceptualizing and measuring youth-adult partnership in community programs: A cross national study", pp. 337–347.

[19] Linda Camino, "Youth-adult partnerships: Entering new territory in community work and research", pp. 11–20.

[20] *Ibid.*

Youth Participation in Singapore

In Singapore, the government recognises the importance of involving youths[21] in community development. Encouraging youth participation is one strategy for nation building, particularly fostering social integration. This is important as Singapore's social landscape is increasingly heterogeneous. In 2017, about three in 10 persons are non-residents, up from one in 10 in 1990.[22]

National priority to develop youths is clear, for example, in the establishment of the National Youth Council in 1989 as the "co-ordinating body for youth affairs in Singapore and the focal point of international youth affairs".[23] The evolution of the Council also shows inroads into youth participation in community development. For example, let us consider the following:

- In 2006, it launched Young ChangeMakers, a grant scheme that supports youth projects that benefit the Singapore community. Youths are the ones who decide which projects to fund and mentor the project applicants.
- In 2013, it set up Youth Corps Singapore — a national movement championing volunteerism among youths founded on the philosophy of service-learning. The movement links youths to volunteering opportunities and trains youth leaders to catalyse collaboration between the other youths and community organisations.

Grassroot organisations have also recognised the need to engage youths for decades. For example, Residents' Committees (RC) and Community Clubs have youth chapters, youth clubs and youth executive committees under the broad umbrella of the People's Association Youth

---

[21] Defined as persons aged 15 to 35 in Singapore.
[22] Department of Statistics, *Population Trends 2017* (Republic of Singapore: Ministry of Trade & Industry, 2017), Retrieved from http://www.singstat.gov.sg/docs/default-source/default-document-library/publications/publications_and_papers/population_and_population_structure/population2017.pdf.
[23] National Youth Council, *Youth.sg: The State of Youth in Singapore 2017 Statistical Handbook* (Singapore: National Youth Council, 2017).

Movement (PAYM). At the tertiary education level, there are many official student-led clubs or societies which promote youth involvement in the community. For example, the National University of Singapore (NUS) Students' Community Services Club (CSC) works closely with different social service organisations (SSOs) to connect their members to a wide range of opportunities to serve the community.

In recent years, aided by mobile technology and social media, Singapore youths are taking the lead in championing community causes. Almost all Singapore youths are Internet users.[24] With ready access to information and resources online, youths who are not satisfied with existing efforts in addressing social concerns by national or community bodies can rally like-minded individuals fairly quickly to design alternative solutions.

The presence of youth-oriented funds such as the Citi-YMCA Youth for Causes Fund and the Young ChangeMakers Grant allows youths with ideas to access the resource they need to champion pet causes. Some of these youth-oriented funds also come with mentors who can guide the applicants in their projects. In addition, with crowdfunding, youths can extend beyond the usual government and corporate channels. These entities, while resource-rich, present more administrative processes for youths requiring funding support than crowdfunding.

While there are no official statistics tracking the degree of youth involvement in community development, a proxy measure can be taken from the National Youth Survey. In 2016, only 10% of Singapore youths aged 15–34 were involved in community social groups and 6% in welfare and self-help social groups.[25] The proportion of youths involved in both social groups is fairly low. Singapore youths, nonetheless, do have an interest to serve their community. More than half of youths aged 15–19 and about 42% of youths aged 20–24 indicated helping the less

---

[24] Infocomm Media Development Authority, Annual Survey on Infocomm Usage in Households and by Individuals for 2015, 2017, Retrieved from https://www.imda.gov.sg/~/media/imda/files/industry%20development/fact%20and%20figures/infocomm%20survey%20reports/2015%20hh%20public%20report%20(120417).pdf?la=en.

[25] National Youth Council, *Youth.sg: The State of Youth in Singapore 2017 Statistical Handbook.*

fortunate and contributing to society as "very important" life goals.[26] This implies that although opportunities for youth involvement in the community abound, more work needs to be done to encourage more youths to bring to fruition their intention to be involved in community development.

Having adult allies who believe and invest in youth-led/youth-initiated programmes is instrumental in facilitating their success.[27] Youths and adults have been partnering in community development in Singapore in varying degrees. On one extreme end of the partnership spectrum, youths are engaged as the "hands and legs" to deliver adult-designed programmes. They provide little or no inputs to the programme design and delivery and have no programme oversights. These typically take place when community organisations require volunteers to play a specific role. Examples of such roles include performing administrative tasks or distributing programme flyers to households.

On the other end, youths design and implement their own community solutions and adults are engaged because of their roles as gatekeepers. These projects are usually short-term and specific such as fund-raising efforts and awareness campaigns by student bodies.

Many community projects lie in the middle of the partnership spectrum because youths who wish to pursue a particular cause usually require access to a target population via community organisations. Community organisations would assign an adult to work with these students to ensure some degree of programme quality and/or adhere to ethics or processes as part of organisational accountability to funders and service users. At Youth Corps Singapore, for example, volunteer leaders-in-training would design and deliver a service-learning programme for a target population in partnership with mentors from SSOs.

While having youths "co-learn" and "co-work" for the betterment of the community is ideal, the realisation of such partnerships is not easy. The following section broadly discusses the challenges of youth participation in community development, including the difficulties in Y–APs.

---

[26] *Ibid.*
[27] Irene Y. H. Ng, "Youth participation: Can we trust youths to lead the community?".

Youth Participation in Community Development: Practical Challenges

The three "isms" highlighted earlier provided attitudinal barriers to youth participation in community development. In this section, we highlight practical challenges. These challenges might ultimately be due to the "isms", as the "isms" lead to not prioritising time and effort to develop Y–AP initiatives and to sort things through in order to make Y–AP work.

Limited Spare Time

In the face of multiple demands on a limited amount of time, youths would prioritise what they consider to be of greater importance. Vasoo observed that the benefits to be gained directly by students from community involvement could be less tangible compared to their other involvements, contributing to a lower than desired rate of community participation. He noted that a higher involvement rate from students and beneficiaries is important to sustain community activities for community problem solving.

Sustainability

In recent years, student-led organisations in schools and communities are becoming more task-centric in their community development efforts — focusing more on organising recreational and socio-educational activities and short-term projects (typically tied to the term of the office bearers).[28] Some projects were outsourced to private contractors as the students had a limited amount of time. The design and implementation of these projects also may not take into account residents' needs. Vasoo voiced his concerns that when youths are too focused on tasks, they may lose touch with residents' needs.

While not all initiatives need to be sustained over time, initiatives which address certain community issues (e.g. mentoring children-at-risk)

---

[28] S Vasoo, "Promoting participation among the young in community development efforts: Issues and challenges".

need to be sustained over a longer time span to see impact. A challenge faced by youths who are developing such programmes is their ability to resource the programme over time — for example, ensuring financial viability, sufficient manpower and leadership succession.

Guidance and Autonomy

As mentioned in earlier segments, avoiding "adultism" does not mean that youths should be left to their own devices. In fact, adult allies matter.[29] Support from adult gatekeepers is instrumental in facilitating youth efforts in community development including granting access to resources, permits and venues, and helping youths navigate institutional processes which can be fairly complex. However, many youths with wonderful ideas to help their communities do not have access to adult allies; or even when they are able to find adult allies or institutional partners, the adults or institutions might provide minimal guidance. At the other extreme, the adults or institutions might find it more convenient to just tell youths what to do, instead of the often more time-consuming route of guiding the process while allowing youths the autonomy to run things. The balance between guidance and autonomy is challenging.

Environmental Constraints

Youths and adults reside in a larger environment that constrains them in many ways. Constraints such as organisational structure, perceptions of cultural norms, processes and rules can facilitate or hinder a Y–AP. The following section illustrates some of these challenges through a case study on a youth-led initiative "STARdy Kaki".

STARdy Kaki: A Case Study

"STARdy Kaki" is an academic support, companionship and character development programme for children from underprivileged families in the Taman Jurong constituency. The programme is a ground-up initiative by

---

[29] Irene Y. H. Ng, "Youth participation: Can we trust youths to lead the community?".

a group of youths, in partnership with "Zone B" RC in Taman Jurong and Fei Yue Family Services (Taman Jurong) (FYFS). The programme comprises a weekly two-hour academic support session with volunteer tutor-mentors who help children with their school work. An hour during every last session of the month, is dedicated to teaching the children values such as perseverance and compassion as part of character development. The programme also includes activities such as outings and parent–tutor meetings to engage children and parents regularly.

The programme was conceptualised initially as a tuition and companionship programme by two students when they were 19 years old. Growing up in Taman Jurong, one student noticed that children from the rental blocks in Taman Jurong had little or no adult supervision and were not performing well academically. She shared her concerns with her good friend, and with support from the RC, the pair started the tuition and companionship programme for these children on a regular basis for free. The RC provided the venue and a small amount of money to kick-start the programme in May 2016. The students had full autonomy in the design and implementation of the trial programme. This experiment on a small scale bolstered their confidence to take the programme further.

FYFS was brought in as a partner to provide professional inputs on developing the programme. Practitioners at FYFS worked with the students to shape the programme, guided them on how they can communicate and work professionally with stakeholders in the community and provided a larger programme venue. This brought about some changes such as the inclusion of the hourly value-based session at the end of each month and programme evaluation. Roles were clearly delineated with the students leading and conducting all components of the programme except for the monthly value-based sessions. Practitioners at FYFS developed and conducted the value-based sessions. FYFS became the main partner for the "STARdy Kaki" programme.

By January 2017, "STARdy Kaki" had a team of more than 20 youths, taking on varying roles such as organising committee members and tutor-mentors. Approximately 20 children from the Taman Jurong community had joined the programme.

The above-mentioned details show the development of a promising YA–P. However, "STARdy Kaki" has also faced the challenges outlined in the previous section. First, the theme of limited spare time was seen in "STARdy Kaki" youth volunteers who exited the programme. Although many reflected their volunteering experience as positive, they had other priorities. For the student leaders who were similarly juggling multiple responsibilities in school, their passion, sense of project ownership and responsibility to the children kept them going.

Second, sustainability was a key challenge, in particular with respect to manpower. A core philosophy for programme quality held by the students is that a small tutor-mentor to children ratio will enhance quality tutoring and mentoring. The programme therefore adhered strictly to not more than two children per tutor-mentor. This implied that the programme required a sizeable number of volunteers to manage weekly operations, holiday and other *ad hoc* activities.

While the student leaders preferred to have a consistent group of tutor-mentors for the children, sustaining a regular pool of peer volunteers proved challenging with attrition. Volunteers recruited may also prefer to commit on an *ad hoc* or short-term basis. The student leaders nonetheless managed to keep to a small tutor-mentor-to-children ratio by recruiting volunteers from various tertiary institutions and their personal networks regularly.

As "STARdy Kaki" relied largely on peer volunteers with similar backgrounds and life stages, this implied that school-to-work transition would happen around the same time. Transiting from school to work tended to reduce the amount of spare time that youths possessed, as their work and adult responsibilities mounted up. Their level of community involvement would consequently be affected. This could impact programme operations if a large number of youths had exited at the same time. Planning for leadership succession and ensuring a diverse pool of volunteers (e.g. youths from other backgrounds, adult or elderly volunteers) was therefore important for youth-led programmes, in view of their life transition.

Fourth, in terms of the balance between guidance and autonomy, the students in "STARdy Kaki" had adult allies who navigated organisational processes on their behalf to facilitate programme implementation such as dealing with internal administrative processes for release of resources (e.g. venues, funds and permits) and managing parents, guardians and children.

Beyond instrumental support, however, the "STARdy Kaki" student leaders reflected that they would like some form of guidance in areas such as managing peer volunteers and a scaled community programme but were unsure about how they should go about asking adults for support without losing their autonomy. At the same time, however, they valued the respect and the autonomy in decision-making as these retained their sense of ownership over the project. "STARdy Kaki" therefore had the characteristic of "authentic decision-making", one of the core elements of Y–AP. Although youths and adult practitioners collectively designed the programme components, the youths in "STARdy Kaki" retained the final decision-making authority. This came about because the youths verbalised their desire to retain the rights over the programme early, and the adult practitioners were able to respect those rights. Thus, the student leaders continued to navigate the balance of continuing with more guidance or more autonomy, and in what aspects of the programme.

Finally, "STARdy Kaki" experienced several environmental constraints. The two youth leaders recounted an incident where an additional academic support session for children taking their Primary School Leaving Examination (PSLE) did not happen because no adult staff from FYFS could be present on the selected date/time, and the organisation had a strict rule that at least one staff must be present for any organisation-related activities involving children for safety and accountability.

While youths believed that parental consent would suffice, the adult practitioners were subjected to, and had to abide by, the rules of the organisation as staff. In this instance, while the organisational rule was sound, the rule affected the partnership. This created some unhappiness among youths and adults alike initially but the good relationship and trust between them allowed the partnership to continue despite the disagreement.

For Y–AP in community development to work effectively, adults need to set aside time to be co-learners and "informal mentors". In "STARdy Kaki", the idea of informal mentorship surfaced during staff meetings but did not fully materialise. Guidance was provided largely in the initial stage of the programme. The practitioners gradually found themselves focusing on the weekly tasks necessary to deliver the programmes for the service users over time.

In short, while there is some degree of adult guidance, the "natural mentorship" element in "STARdy Kaki" can be strengthened. "Reciprocal activity" in terms of co-learning and "community connectedness" are not evident. These are elements that have to be purposefully incorporated in the future.

Recommendations

Helping youths actualise their intention may contribute to increasing the proportion of youths involved in community development. This meant that barriers to participation should be reduced where possible. This section suggests some ways of encouraging youth participation and youth–adult partnerships for community development.

Engaging Occasional Volunteers Meaningfully

While the issue of limited spare time is not easily resolved, efforts can be made to make the small pockets of time provided by youths count. While regular volunteerism among youths is preferred and should be encouraged for the benefits it brings, it may be worthwhile for community organisations to relook at engaging youths who volunteer occasionally meaningfully. Volunteer roles and management practices can be reviewed for more meaningful engagement without compromising long-term community development. For example, with technology, notions of "participation" and "community" for youths have extended beyond the physical to online spaces. If volunteering roles can be restructured, youths with pockets of time can volunteer where they are, without being physically present.

Addressing Sustainability Issues

Embracing diversity. Structures can be created to ensure that a diverse group of youths can be represented in various community groups (including youths who may be the subject of community efforts, be from minority groups or with disabilities). Engaging youths who are subject of community efforts, in particular, allows them to go beyond being passive recipients. Youths do not have to be top students or the best of their cohorts. They should be engaged based on their interest and ability to serve their community. This helps address issues of elitism.

Intentional efforts must be made to engage, train and mentor these youths with a heart to serve for the purpose of grooming them for long-term community leadership. This rejuvenates community leadership in an ageing population. For youth-led groups, succession planning ensures that the skills and experience gained by existing youth leaders can be transferred to younger and other types of youths in a structured manner.[30]

Including some adult or elderly volunteers in youth-led initiatives may also be helpful not only for reducing operational risks but also for the knowledge, skills and networks that these adults or elderly possess which may lend insights and support for programme development. This will nonetheless lead to another set of challenges for youth leaders as managing a diverse volunteer pool beyond peers may not be something that they are familiar with.

Encouraging Youth–Adult Partnership

The importance of adult allies in youth participation cannot be overemphasised and their support facilitates youth participation.[31] Adult allies need to guide without being "adultist", and this may be possible when they adopt the stance of a co-learner in the spirit of Y–AP. The act of balancing guidance and preserving youth autonomy, however, is more an art than a science. It involves open communication between youths and adults and a willingness to trust and learn from each other.

Y–AP may be a good way forward in encouraging youth participation in community development. The core elements in the conceptual model proposed by Zeldin *et al.*, that is, "authentic decision-making, natural mentors, reciprocal activity, and community connectedness" remind adult

---

[30] *Ibid.*
[31] *Ibid.*

gatekeepers that youths can contribute and they should be involved.[32] They also remind everyone involved that partnership is a two-way street and that the voice of beneficiaries must be heard. For Y–AP to happen in practice, however, community organisations need to make a deliberate effort to adapt the existing work processes.

Shier's Pathways to Participation offers a model which organisations can use to assess and ready themselves for youth participation.[33] The model includes the following five levels of participation:

(1) listen to youths;
(2) support youths in expressing their views;
(3) take youths' views into account;
(4) involve youths in decision-making;
(5) share power and responsibility for decision-making with youths.

For each level, Shier proposes three stages of readiness. The opening stage creates the environment for that level of youth participation; at the opportunity stage, there are sufficient knowledge and resources to start youth participation; and at the obligation stage, that level of youth participation becomes an agreed policy in the organisation.

For organisations who are ready to do so, some areas of process adaptations are suggested:

Investing Time. Investing time is necessary for Y–AP to work. Organisations with an interest in partnering youths for community development have to ensure that the practitioners have the time to engage and guide as a "natural mentor", actively co-learn as part of "reciprocal activity" and share community networks ("community connectedness").[34] This may require organisations to make changes to internal processes to

---

[32] Shepherd Zeldin, Brian D. Christens and Jane L. Powers, "The psychology and practice of youth-adult partnership: Bridging generations for youth development and community change", pp. 385–397.

[33] Harry Shier, "Pathways to participation: Openings, opportunities and obligations", *Children and Society*, 15(2), 2001, pp. 107–117.

[34] Shepherd Zeldin, Brian D. Christens and Jane L. Powers, "The psychology and practice of youth-adult partnership: Bridging generations for youth development and community change", pp. 385–397.

facilitate Y–AP. One example is the relooking at manpower planning to create space for the staff to guide, and learn from, youths.

Facilitating Regular Reflection. Regular and respectful communication was highlighted as critical in building trust, reconciling differences and aligning expectations among youths and practitioners in "STARdy Kaki". The good relationship built allowed them to weather differences in opinions. Regular communication is therefore important in building strong relationships.

Camino proposed the use of reflecting regularly during meetings as a tool to move Y–AP forward in practice.[35] Reflection allows youths and adults to: (i) listen to one another; (ii) agree on collaboration outcomes; (iii) clarify positions and roles held and (iv) clarify how the collaboration benefits youths, adults and the community. The drawing up of a programme model with its theories of change was recommended as helpful in guiding the discussions, especially in defining collaboration outcomes. For the facilitation process, Camino also recommended engaging a third party to help reach clarity and consensus.[36]

Regular reflection will be a very helpful tool for developing youths and adults involved in Y–AP. This helps address issues such as insufficient adult guidance as youths and adults involved will have regular conversations on existing challenges faced. This allows for co-creation of community solutions. The inclusion of beneficiaries' voices in programme design and implementation needs to take place such that they are no longer passive recipients. This prevents situations of learned helplessness within the community in the long run.

Developing a Y–AP Practice Framework

With the emphasis on encouraging youths' active involvement in the community, and the interest in sustaining their engagement, it may be good to start researching youth–adult partnership practices locally with the aim of developing a Y–AP practice framework over time. The practice of Y–AP

---

[35] Linda Camino, "Pitfalls and promising practices of youth-adult partnerships: An evaluator's reflections", pp. 75–85.
[36] *Ibid.*

is not well documented in Singapore as Y–AP is hardly discussed or researched. Organisations pursuing Y–AP, nonetheless, can contribute by documenting and sharing their best practices as a start.

Conclusion

Youths need adult allies who are willing to be their partners in community development. Co-learning and sharing resources including access to networks allow youths and adults to co-create community solutions. The partnership will be helpful in addressing adultism and it allows the voices of youths and adults (including beneficiaries) to be heard. Y–AP is not a miracle pill that removes all barriers of youth participation in the community. It is, however, an important type of community development partnership that can yield greater good for all. For Y–AP to flourish, organisations need to be willing to set aside resources to experiment and innovate and document challenges, failures and best practices in their Y–AP journey. This will contribute to the development of a Y–AP practice framework over time.

Chapter 9

Bakery Hearts: Lessons in the Intersections of Community Work and Social Entrepreneurship

Elisha Paul Teo and Sheean Chia

Introduction

The fundamental similarity between community development practices in social work practice and social entrepreneurship is the emphasis of "the community" as the site of intervention and development of existing resources to expand social and economic capacities.[1] The goal of community development practices in social work can be summarised in three key constructs: (1) empowering people, (2) encouraging participation and (3) building social capital to promote change in their communities.[2] Social

---

[1] Monica Nandan, Manuel London and Terry C. Blum, "Community practice social entrepreneurship: An interdisciplinary approach to graduate education", *International Journal of Social Entrepreneurship and Innovation*, 3(1), 2014, pp. 51–70.

[2] Lionel J. Beaulieu, "Mapping the assets of your community: A key component for building local capacity", SRDC Series #227, 2002, Retrieved from http://srdc.msstate.edu/publications/227/227_asset_mapping.pdf.

enterprises, on the other hand, pride themselves on their entrepreneurial aptitude to meet social needs in a sustainable manner.[3] Though a stark difference exists between organic services (community-centric) and design services (organisation-driven), both social entrepreneurship and community work do transcend into similar spaces of empowerment and sustainability.

Social enterprises have been heralded as a viable social development strategy to provide gainful employment to vulnerable communities.[4] It is in this capacity that social entrepreneurship may complement and value-add to current community development practices. The present sphere of community work we observe today revolves more towards the formation and reinforcement of informal social networks — people become neighbours, neighbours become friends and friends become resources. However, for communities that struggle with socio-economic challenges of financial self-sufficiency and employment opportunities, the incremental strengthening of social networks may not necessarily translate into sustainable social change.

An alternative option may be for social enterprises that champion work integration business models, to partner with social workers to increase accessibility to economic resources. With the consistent engagement of social workers with the community at the family service sector, communities can be directed to vocational training social enterprises or work opportunities that correspond to their identified assets (asset mapping and matching).

This chapter discusses how community-based social workers uniquely engage in social entrepreneurship as a method of community work development. An illustration of Bakery Hearts, a programme under Ang Mo Kio Family Service Centre (AMKFSC) Community Services Ltd., will be used to discuss the overlapping modalities of both social entrepreneurship and community work. The authors will discuss the challenges of

---

[3] B Lab, "Bettr Barista Pte Ltd. B Impact Report", 2018, Retrieved from https://bcorporation.net/directory/bettr-barista.

[4] Jonathan Chang, "Commentary: The power of Singapore's social entrepreneurs in a profit-driven world", 2017, Retrieved from https://www.channelnewsasia.com/news/singapore/commentary-the-power-of- singapore-s-social-entrepreneurs-in-a-9085494.

managing the programme within the larger landscape of social enterprises in Singapore.

Community Development and Social Enterprise — The Unique Position of Social Workers

Nandan *et al.* called on social workers to engage in social entrepreneurship as one of the methods of social innovation to creatively tackle social issues.[5] Both practices value collaborations with the residents and clients in the process of identifying, designing and developing services and programmes to empower community residents to take ownership to resolve social issues. Such practices accentuate the core values of social work practice and social entrepreneurship to uphold the client's self-determination and empowerment of marginalised communities. These approaches, both in the contexts, have been proven to be effective in ensuring the sustainability of the programme or services as residents are deemed as the experts of the situation, and not the social worker or the entrepreneur.

The Bakery Hearts Programme, a project initiated by the AMKFSC Community Services Ltd., may illustrate the synergy between community development theories and modalities and the spirit of social entrepreneurship in addressing employment challenges faced by women of low-income families. Social work's embrace of community development theory and practice provides an important foundation from which to explore the relevance of social enterprises to social work.[6]

The Bakery Hearts Endeavours

The Bakery Hearts Programme, one of the community services initiated by AMKFSC in 2011, aims to support the needs of unemployed women from

---

[5] Monica Nandan, Manuel London and Tricia Bent-Goodley, "Social workers as social change agents: Social innovation, social intrapreneurship, and social entrepreneurship", *Human Service Organizations: Management, Leadership & Governance*, 39(1), 2015, pp. 38–56.
[6] Mel Gray, Karen Healy and Penny Crofts, "Social enterprise: Is it the business of social work?" *Australian Social Work*, 56, 2003, pp. 141–154.

low-income families. It seeks to empower and provide women with baking and social skills to prepare them for eventual integration or reintegration into regular employment or into the workforce.[7] The programme also provides income-generating opportunities, where profits made from the sales of the baked goods will be shared among all the participants. During their period of participation, psychoeducational and support groups will be implemented by the social workers to build up participants' skills capacity and self-confidence.

The programme hopes not only for women to be able to gain eventual employment but also for them to lay the groundwork in building up their social networks to reduce social isolation, as well as their financial assets (that is, savings). The social enterprise framework mirrors the values of social work practice and fits with theories of community development.

Bakery Hearts's Social Entrepreneurship and Community Development

Definitions and cause of social enterprises

It appears that there is no standard international definition of a social enterprise.[8] In the United Kingdom, social enterprises are defined as "businesses" which explicitly aim "to improve personal and collective well-being in reducing inequalities and increasing social cohesion, as well as benefiting the community, mainly through creation of decent jobs for marginalised and excluded people, reintegration of people with difficulties into the labour market, provision and delivery of collective goods and social services for low income individuals, increase of social capital and dissemination of social innovations". However, according to the guide published by Singapore's Social Enterprise Association, social enterprises have been defined as follows:

---

[7] Mohamed Fareez Bin Mohamed Fahmy and Lee Sin Yan, *The Bakery Hearts Project: A Phenomenological Study on the Experiences of Low-Income Women Participants of a Social Enterprise* (Singapore: Ang Mo Kio Family Service Centres, 2011).

[8] Mak Yuen Teen, *Primer on Governance for Social Enterprises in Singapore* (Singapore: Social Enterprise Association Ltd., 2013).

1. They are designed specifically to address certain social, cultural and/or environmental issues.
2. It declares this mission in its constitution or declares it publicly if it has no constitution.
3. It uses business strategies and activities to tackle its stated mission.
4. It generates and distributes its revenue and surpluses to achieve its stated mission.[9]

The models of social enterprises in Singapore can be broadly classified into: (1) work integration model, (2) plough-back-profit model, (3) subsidised services model and (4) social needs model. The work integration model identifies disadvantaged populations in the society and provides them with skills training or employment opportunities with the clear intentions of integrating them back to society. In contrast, the plough-back-profit model proposes a social enterprise that typically generates income to fund their affiliated charities and social programmes. Meanwhile, a social enterprise that adopts the subsidised services model creates a service which provides subsidised rates for the disadvantaged population identified while mainstream customers will pay commercial rates due to higher purchasing power. Lastly, the social needs model seeks to address specific societal issues through the designing of programmes.[10]

The Bakery Hearts programme could be categorised as a work integration model as its mission is to support women to seek eventual employment in the private sector, where profits and surpluses are shared with the participants during their term in the programme. Notably, social enterprises are not expected to survive on donations and are able to rely on a business model to be self-sustaining. Hence, one will be able to observe that the Bakery Hearts programme overlaps between the functions of a social enterprise and those of a social service organisation.[11] The following segment will discuss on the theories and modalities behind the conceptualisation of the programme.

---

[9] *Ibid.*
[10] *Ibid.*
[11] *Ibid.*

Theories and Modalities for Community Development in Bakery Hearts

Needs assessment

In community work practice, it is necessary to conduct needs assessment to understand the extent of a problem with a client population in a community. It is considered the first step in responding to the perceived needs and a vital step in programme development.[12] It aims to identify whether there have been barriers for clients and/or communities in accessing needs and services. However, over the years, there have been calls for practitioners to shift perspective, or to adopt perspective, of both "Needs-based Analysis" and the "Asset-based Analysis".

The Asset-Based Community Development (ABCD) approach

The ABCD approach, founded by McKnight and Kretzmann, has been widely adopted by community workers in the recent years as the guiding principles in their community-building efforts.[13] This approach has gained widespread attention as it challenges the traditional approach of a Needs-based Analysis of a community, which focuses on mapping and assessing the deficits and problems that plagued the community, to an Asset-based Analysis, which believes in identifying and strengthening the existing community's strengths and assets.[14] Additionally, the conventional approach seems to posit that the service providers and funding agencies should take on responsibilities in solving the issues in the community while the ABCD approach strives to debunk the notion, believing that "community assets are key building blocks in sustainable urban and rural community revitalization efforts".[15]

---

[12] David Royse, Bruce A. Thyer and Deborah K. Padgett, *Program Evaluation: An Introduction* (Australia: Wadsworth Cengage Learning, 2010).
[13] John McKnight and John Kretzmann, *Mapping Community Capacity* (PDF) (Report), Revised edn. (Evanston, IL: Northwestern University Institute for Policy Research, 1996).
[14] Hanna Nel, "A comparison between the asset-oriented and needs-based community development approaches in terms of systems changes", *Practice*, 30(1), 2018, pp. 33–52.
[15] ABCD Institute: Founders, 2001–2018, Retrieved from DePaul University, Asset-Based Community Development Institute: https://resources.depaul.edu/abcd-institute/about/founders/Pages/default.aspx.

Broadly, at the core of the ABCD approach, it identifies six forms of assets. First, it is to identify the gifts of individuals in the community — the skill sets, talents and experiences of residents (i.e. plumbing, singing, caring for elderly, strong interest in volunteering, etc.), the local individual and home-based business (that is, hawker centres, grocery shops, home bakers and cooks, etc.) and organically forged relationships among the residents.[16] The residents, in this approach, are the greatest asset. Second, it is to identify the residents' managed organisations and associations (that is, religious groups, interest groups, etc.). Ultimately, it is for networks to be built among the residents, businesses and associations to increase their self-interest and expand their vision in taking ownership in developing their own community.[17] Third, it is to identify the private, non-profit organisations (that is, private business, social service institutions, etc.), public institutions and services (that is, public schools, police, etc.) and to involve them creatively in community development ideas. Next, it is to identify the physical and economic resources (that is, the infrastructures, untapped land, utilities, etc.) in the community. The idea behind this is to build partnerships with the owners of these assets to utilise the spaces effectively for community projects. Moving on, it is to identify the natural exchanges among the resources — the interactions of the residents with the assets mentioned above. Lastly, it is to capture the stories, histories of residents' experiences in the community, strengthening the culture and identity of the residents.[18]

The Bakery Hearts programme has been founded on several of these principles. Coupled with the work-integration model from the social enterprise's perspective, the programme strives to be a uniquely viable and sustainable income-generating community intervention for clients within the locality of the Family Service Centre (FSC).

---

[16] John McKnight, *A Basic Guide to ABCD Community Organizing* (Detroit, MI: Asset-Based Community Development Institute, 2013).
[17] *Ibid.*
[18] John McKnight, *Asset-Based Community Development: The Essentials* (Detroit, MI: Asset-Based Community Development Institute, 2017).

The Design of Bakery Hearts

Needs assessments

Bakery Hearts, founded in 2011, was based on the evident trends obtained from the statistics from the casework, as well as the felt and expressed needs of women from disadvantaged families and the social workers working with this profile of clients. These needs are further backed up by secondary analysis — with vast research and literature discussing on the women being more susceptible to poverty due to the limited opportunities and options for them, presenting challenges for them to break the cycle.[19]

Financial challenge remains as the top pressing issue for clients to seek support from the FSC.[20] It is often tied in closely with employment concerns, particularly in Singapore, where Singaporeans have been accustomed to the idea of generating income through gainful and long period of employment as a benchmark to ensure self-reliance. However, underlying this challenge are multifaceted barriers at the individual and family levels as well the economic climate and business structures that do not support women seeking and/or sustaining gainful employment.

Fareez and Lee had conducted a qualitative study on the women who were in Bakery Hearts by adopting semi-structured interviews.[21] Findings had shown that one of the main barriers for women seeking employment were caregiving responsibilities, something that may be highly influenced by the cultural roles ascribed to women. The interviewees from this study expressed that despite the low income that the family is earning, the family's cultural and religious beliefs supported perceptions that women should not be working and should take on the role of the main caregiver for their children.

---

[19] Association of Women for Action and Research, "Why are you not working? Low-income mothers explain challenges with work & care", 2018, Retrieved from https://www.aware.org.sg/reports/.
[20] AMKFSC Community Services Ltd, Annual Report FY2017, 2017, Retrieved from https://www.amkfsc.org.sg/publications/category/2-annual-reports.
[21] Mohamed Fareez Bin Mohamed Fahmy and Lee Sin Yan, *The Bakery Hearts Project: A Phenomenological Study on the Experiences of Low-Income Women Participants of a Social Enterprise.*

Meanwhile, another challenge that the women faced in seeking employment was to balance their caregiving demands and work responsibilities with the long shift hours and limited leave benefits. Most of the women had only a low level of education, ranging between primary school and secondary school levels, posing it as a challenge for them to gain employment with higher salary, which is often accompanied by higher benefits such as annual and childcare leaves. The skills that these women possessed, such as baking or cleaning, exposed them to industries (that is, retail, food and beverage) that usually require them to commit to long working hours and shift work. Coupled with the cultural factor, it posed as a deterrent in gaining and sustaining of employment for women.

Hence, one of the crucial designs that the Bakery Hearts programme possesses is the flexibility provided for the participants. Women get to choose the days that they can commit to the programme, and the timing for baking is arranged while their children are attending schools, childcare or after-school care. This unique arrangement in the programme is termed as "preferential flexployment". From the study, the women had expressed that they appreciated such arrangements, where they could balance between the caregiving and household demands, while earning some form of remuneration.

The ABCD Approach of Bakery Hearts

Gifts of the programme

The formation of the Bakery Hearts programme comes from the identification of the gifts that the women bring with them. Through the existing casework and community work process, social workers identified the gifts of the women which include a strong interest in cooking, baking, handicrafts, sewing and so on. In order to standardise the processes and operations, baking was chosen as a tool to develop their skills for eventual reintegration to the workforce.

The physical asset

With the gifts of the residents and the purpose of the social cause identified, the support of the relevant community stakeholders has to be garnered to aid and to realise the vision of the programme. The priority was to secure a venue with baking facilities to support the baking operations of the programme. The unique position of the community social worker comes with an ecological perspective, as well as the role of a broker in utilising the necessary resources in the community to locate and work with stakeholders within the community. An important stakeholder in supporting social and community needs is the community centre (CC), which is equipped with facilities to provide residents with meaningful programmes that promote social bonding.[22] One of the facilities included is the cooking and baking kitchen; the CCs in Ang Mo Kio also provide cooking and/or baking classes for the residents.

In order to secure a permanent location for the programme, Bakery Hearts thus initiated a network with the Community Centre Management Committee (CCMC) to explore partnership for the programme to rent the kitchen facilities in the CCs. Despite several challenges that arose across the years in securing a permanent location in the CCs due to the mismatch of expectations in the partnerships, Bakery Hearts eventually, through the strong support of the grassroots, set up its central baking kitchen in the Ang Mo Kio Community Centre (AMKCC).

Interest from public and private institutions

As Bakery Hearts is a transitional programme in nature, there is a need to ensure the consistency of the baked goods as well as to innovate or learn new products. During the initial phase of the programme, it tapped on social networks within the community to recruit volunteers to conduct baking trainings. These volunteers were mainly skilled home bakers and people who were willing to share their gifts to contribute to the cause of the programme.

As the programme further developed, partnerships were forged with private corporations who expressed a keen interest in supporting the development of Bakery Hearts. An important intermediary in this process was the National Council of Social Service (NCSS), which supported the

---

[22] Singapore Infopedia, 16 October 2013, Retrieved from http://eresources.nlb.gov.sg/infopedia/articles/SIP_2013-10-18_183012.html.

matching between the expectations of the private organisations that expressed interest to develop corporate social responsibilities (CSR) and the needs of the Social Service Organisations (SSOs). At present, Bakery Hearts has forged strong partnerships with the Pan Pacific Hotels Group and Suntec Singapore. Both corporations are committed in providing various opportunities for the participants under the programme such as booth sales and kitchen tours. Pan Pacific Hotels Group, in particular, has been focusing on providing consultancy support on operations management and uplifting the baking skills of the participants through regular training.

In summary, the Bakery Hearts programme has been able to make significant progress across the years through applying the ABCD guiding principles. There have been conscious efforts in engaging stakeholders in the communities in various levels. Meanwhile, the usage of social media in marketing the programme has also allowed Bakery Hearts to gain more interest among the socially conscious consumers and corporates over the years. However, there also lie challenges in managing the programme, given its unique nature.

The Challenges Faced by Bakery Hearts

Forging identities and culture

The last principle of the ABCD approach seeks to strengthen the identity and ownership of the participants through the capturing of stories. However, due to the transitional nature of the programme where participants have different lengths in participation periods, it is a challenge to forge a sense of common identity. To counter this, social workers apply group-work theories for intentionally setting time to include the participants in verbalising and sharing about programme-related matters, as well as working towards a common goal of addressing challenges in seeking for employment. Moving forward, there will be efforts to document the stories of participants who have successfully graduated from the programme collaboratively.

Income-generating and sustaining programme

Meanwhile, a constant challenge that is faced by the Bakery Hearts programme is the ability to generate and sustain profits while meeting the social cause. In order to meet the profit margins to sustain the operations of the programme, it assumes that there will be a stable group of manpower to meet the demands of the products. However, participants in the programme manage multiple roles and responsibilities. Hence, given the daily stressors, participation to the programme could be irregular as they are expected to manage the family crisis. Yet, as a training programme, there is a need to strike a balance between meeting the social goals of allocating sufficient time to build up personal and group competencies in seeking for employment and fulfilling the financial demands of the programme. For Bakery Hearts, a training programme set up by a charity organisation, profits are still necessary to ensure sustainability while consistent and/or additional funding is also important to cushion the unpredictability of the sales and manpower of the programme. Yet at a macro-level, these challenges are also experienced across local social enterprises and it will be further explained in the following section.

Challenges Faced in Using Social Enterprises in Community Development

Based on the report by the Singapore Centre for Social Enterprise, 66% of those engaged in social entrepreneurship are doing so for the first time.[23] With the volatility of the market and no assurance of success, being able to generate income and recoup the capital can be extremely challenging. Profits can help cushion social enterprises from economic volatility, retain talent and grow their business model to better meet their social mission.[24]

Therefore, there is a need for a viable business model that is profitable with a clearly defined social mission, unique value proposition and shared good practices within the industry as they remain key for the social enterprises to be sustainable. It is paramount then to ensure that there is adequate support and targeted benefits for the aspiring social entrepreneurs. However,

---

[23] raiSE, 2018, Retrieved from https://www.raise.sg/social-enterprises/social-enterprises-menu/stories.html.
[24] Jonathan Chang, "Commentary: The power of Singapore's social entrepreneurs in a profit-driven world".

even with adequate funding, human capital remains an issue. Part of the challenge in employing clients for social enterprises is that agencies have to make concessions to accommodate the caregiving needs or home emergencies faced by clients. Clients' retention at work is an issue that might require some study by social researchers, apart from some investigations.

Similar to profit and funding, human talent is also essential in social enterprises. It was found that 83% of the social enterprises stay operational for less than 3 years.[25] One of the key reasons is that it is difficult to attract and retain talent. Typically, in a social enterprise, salary cannot be compared to the corporate sectors. In addition, due to the unstable nature of social enterprises, there is no strong sense of job security. This creates a vicious cycle then, where no or little talent enter and remain in the social enterprises, and due to lack of talent, sustainability in terms of having enough people and the right people becomes an issue and this ultimately leads to the inability to generate profits and remain self-sustaining. After all, setting up a business is not an easy task. Without the necessary guidance and resources, failure is inevitable.

Furthermore, there may be a lack of understanding of the mechanisms of social entrepreneurship and social enterprises in Singapore. Often people avoid the social sector as it is associated with financial sacrifices, or that the profit should not be given to the social entrepreneurs and be solely directed to the beneficiaries.[26] This also poses an issue as common people on the street may come under the impression that these are charity organisations and are not for profit. The lack of understanding leads to wrong expectations of these social enterprises, which ultimately leads to a lack of support. These then perpetuate the problem of hiring and creating a sustainable business model with enough human capital.[27]

---

[25] Prethika Nair, "Social enterprises, a possible cure for the world's societal problems?", 2017, Retrieved from https://lkyspp.nus.edu.sg/gia/article/social-enterprises-a-possible-cure-for-the-world-s-societal-problems.

[26] Jonathan Chang, "Commentary: The power of Singapore's social entrepreneurs in a profit-driven world".

[27] Tang See Kit, "Good businesses: Meet the entrepreneurs who want to make Singapore a better place", 2017, Retrieved from https://www.channelnewsasia.com/news/singapore/good-businesses-meet-the-entrepreneurs-who-want-to-make-9513238.

However, despite these challenges, according to the Thomson Reuters Foundation 2016, it was found that Singapore ranked fourth as one of the best places to be a social entrepreneur.[28] Between 2013 and 2014, it is reported that there was a 30% increase in the total number of social enterprises in Singapore.[29] A significant number of initiatives were set up in view of how the government and community leaders saw social enterprises as beneficial to Singapore. Ministry of Social and Family Development (MSF) had set up funds and tax policies to benefit social enterprise start-ups and encourage larger social enterprises to come to Singapore. In 2003, ComCare Enterprise Fund was set up to provide seed funding for social enterprises. In 2009, Social Enterprise Association was created to promote and raise awareness of the social enterprises. The Social Enterprise Hub was also set up as a community for social enterprises to synergise and leverage on one another. And beyond all these, there are encouragements for corporate traditional businesses to put more emphasis on CSR and to create social impacts even though they are largely profit-driven. By 2012, enough traction was formed that the President Office created the President Challenge Social Enterprise Award to recognise outstanding social enterprises for their positive social impact on the community.[30]

It is further recommended that additional education be provided to the general public. Information and knowledge of social enterprises should be more widely publicised with possible roadshows to explain the existing policies aiding social enterprises and also serve as an educational booth for the general public, to better understand and support the existing social enterprises and for the upcoming and budding ones. Recognising that there are some educational institutes like the Singapore Management University and Lee Kuan Yew School of Public Policy that offer courses

---

[28] NCSS, Social service sector strategic thrusts, 2017, Retrieved from https://www.ncss.gov.sg/4st; raiSE, The state of social enterprise in Singapore, 2017, Retrieved from https://www.raise.sg/images/resources/pdf-files/raiSE---State-of-Social-Enterprise-in-Singapore-2017-Report.pdf.
[29] Priscilla Goy, "With social enterprises, more doing good while doing business", *The Straits Times*, 15 September 2014.
[30] Prethika Nair, "Social enterprises, a possible cure for the world's societal problems?".

and electives on social entrepreneurship and social enterprises, perhaps educational institutes could consider introducing social enterprise as a subject to secondary or pre-tertiary education institutes, so that the exposure starts early.[31]

Social Worker's Challenges in Performing Multiple Roles in Social Entrepreneurship and Community Development

Social workers helming community development and social entrepreneurship initiatives play many roles to ensure that a programme like Bakery Hearts would achieve the positive outcomes they have set out to accomplish. From being a programme planner and coordinator to playing the role of a logistician, to acting as a recruiter and ensuring that the programme's clerical administration is properly followed through, social workers still seek to ensure that their daily duties of attending to clients for casework and arranging group work for suitable clients are not neglected. Given that social workers might not possess all the expertise of managing a social enterprise, more time is required for them to read up and be kept up-to-date on new government policies and developments. While this might pose a challenge for social workers to take on further projects to explore and innovate how they can help their clients and better serve the community, it also opens up possibilities for social workers to consider seeking the existing social enterprises in the marketplace to explore possible collaborations. Social enterprises needing manpower could tap on the social workers to be their Employability Ambassadors, as these workers are often involved in conversations with the clients through casework and counselling. However, as the nature of the clients' and communities' issues have been predicted to be increasingly complex in the 21st century, social workers are also faced with the issue of how they are able to respond to these challenges innovatively as they engage in social entrepreneurship.[32]

---

[31] *Ibid.*

[32] Andrew J. Germak and Karun K. Singh, "Social entrepreneurship: Changing the way social workers do business", *Administration in Social Work*, 34(1), 2009, pp. 79–95.

Conclusion

In conclusion, if social workers only work at an individual/micro level, it will be hard to create a platform for their clients to be able to give back to the community. This would only result in the clients staying at a level where they would be perceived as passive recipients of services and not be presented with the opportunity of giving back as an active contributor to their communities. However, if social workers are proactive in identifying residents' skills, gifts and talents, regardless of their age, gender, race and ethnic background, they could engage the residents actively in roles to address important local matters.[33]

This chapter has discussed extensively on how social entrepreneurship could be one of the upcoming creative modalities in community development in social work practice. According to Lawler and Bilson, there have been calls for social work practitioners to take up leadership in bringing about lasting social impacts on communities and in the lives of their clients.[34] While it seems that social entrepreneurship could be a good way to bring about such lasting social change where the community at large gets to feel the impact rather than just the social work's clients, it would make more economic sense for the social workers to partner with the existing social enterprises to ensure that there will be more sustainability in such joint collaborations.[35]

---

[33] Lionel J. Beaulieu, "Mapping the assets of your community: A key component for building local capacity".

[34] John Lawler and Andy Bilson, *Social Work Management and Leadership: Managing Complexity with Creativity* (London: Routledge, 2010).

[35] Monica Nandan, Manuel London and Tricia Bent-Goodley, "Social workers as social change agents: Social innovation, social intrapreneurship, and social entrepreneurship", pp. 38–56.

Chapter 10

From "Homeless" to Survivalist: A Journey in Community Organising

Chan Xian Jie

Introduction

It was 7.30 in the evening as dinner was starting around a pavilion at East Coast Park (ECP). A mat was laid out with a small spread of food as people gathered amidst the sounds of waves gently crashing onto the shoreline, with avid runners and cyclists passing by. Dinner conversations started about how their days had been, before going into more serious discussions about current life situations, dilemmas and challenges. This monthly gathering at ECP, one of the most popular outdoor recreational spots in Singapore, was not a leisurely meetup among friends, but a community meeting among social workers and a group of survivalists who have been staying in the park due to housing challenges.

Community work and the organising of a social work practice method have been underemphasised in the social service sector in Singapore. Such efforts are typically left to other sectors such as the grassroots network and Community Development Councils (CDCs), which tend to focus on social activities or run task-oriented programmes. Few voluntary welfare organisations based in the community, delve into the daily struggles of the socially excluded, oppressed or vulnerable communities to work jointly with them for social change.

Within the Family Service Centres (FSCs) in Singapore, there have been recent sector-wide changes which seemed to further focus on the importance of case management practices through the introduction of various assessment tools or frameworks for social work practice. Funding and operating models have also been modified to incorporate these new practices. This development renews questions on what the roles and functions of social workers in Singapore society are and how they are operationalised. While case management is, without a doubt, an important competency in social work practice, is it the only defining cornerstone that identifies the profession? How would the other social work intervention modalities fit in within the current context of Singapore?

The social work mission is guided through its values, and one of the key values is social justice.[1] Hardcastle *et al.* see social justice in social work as indispensable, a *raison d'être* of social work.[2] As such, the engagement of communities, especially the oppressed and disenfranchised, should be a key task of social workers. The underemphasis of this in the Singapore context brings to mind Specht and Courtney's discussion on how social work has perhaps abandoned its mission of improving vulnerable communities and moved towards individualised psychotherapy interventions.[3]

In light of the continuing developments in the Singapore context, do such tensions of losing sight of the mission of social work exist? If so, how can we better shape our services to remain committed to the mission of social work? This chapter attempts to further consider this dilemma, through the example of working with homelessness in Singapore, while offering a potential model for community development, based on the

---

[1] Singapore Association of Social Workers, Singapore association of social workers code of professional ethics, 2017, Retrieved from https://www.sasw.org.sg/docs/SASW%20Code%20of%20Professional%20Ethics%20-%203rd%20Revision%20(online).pdf.
[2] David A. Hardcastle, Patricia R. Powers and Stanley Wenocur, *Community Practice: Theories and Skills for Social Workers*, 3rd edn. (Oxford: Oxford University Press, 2011).
[3] Harry Specht and Mark E. Courtney, *Unfaithful Angels: How Social Work Has Abandoned Its Mission* (New York, NY: Free Press, 1994).

collectivisation and facilitation of the oppressed, to take action in improving social conditions for themselves.

Homelessness in Singapore

Homelessness has usually been a hot-button topic met with a variety of reactions and responses across Singapore society. In public discourse, people facing homelessness are often politicised by various sections and framed negatively, with the genuineness of their situation frequently put into question. There are those who jump on the bandwagon and further blame the "homeless" people for their plight and for making poor decisions. Simultaneously, there are also advocates and sympathisers who question the affordability of housing, stringent public housing eligibility criteria and other system barriers faced by those with housing challenges.

Political Society

The ongoing debates about homelessness brings to mind Chaterjee's term, *political* society, which was coined to understand the dynamics of certain identified groups whose existence verged on the margins of legality.[4] These groups are often described with empirically or statistically defined characteristics and are also the target of policies and social interventions.[5] Homelessness has been a frequent feature in Singapore parliament and political websites, with questions asked over the years about the extent of the issue, the profile of such groups, how it is being dealt with and also explaining how their challenges came about.

However, these ongoing debates on homelessness seldom involve those who are deemed "homeless" themselves. Cases are often quoted, but their voices and thoughts are often not heard in most discussions. This was pointed out by Chatterjee, who believes that members of political society are often not regarded as proper citizens possessing rights nor do they

---

[4] Partha Chatterjee, "Democracy and economic transformation in India", *Economic & Political Weekly*, 43(16), 2008, pp. 53–62.
[5] *Ibid.*

belong in the civil society, and thus, they will struggle to put forward claims and effectively negotiate for their rights and entitlements.[6] This process is observed in not only the daily struggles of those facing housing issues but also on how the narrative of homelessness is framed in Singapore's society.

Framing of Identity

In the public sphere, being "homeless" comes with many associations and stereotypes, such as being lazy, dirty, crazy, vagrant, unmotivated and uncooperative. These negative labels present in the public realm are often projections put forth by dominant groups in society, onto people living in the streets, to explain this phenomenon. This process essentially others them, creates differences and allows us to continue to politicise their situation and further dehumanise them.

Identity within social services

This othering process is not limited to public realms alone. Many who are experiencing homelessness seek social services for assistance, where these negative identities are often replayed. When engaging with systems that are involved in addressing homelessness, most tend to only engage on a singular case basis, rather than a discussion of homelessness as a pervasive social issue. A case-based conversation frequently drifts to the housing options one has, based on their family and housing history, assets and resources. These options are often formulated without the consultation of the very individuals themselves. When these individuals do not agree, they are then described as resistant and deviant, even though some of these options are not realistic or even of interest to them.

These labels are then generalised across to others who also have housing challenges and who mostly are lazy and unmotivated to work on their challenges. As a result, a dominant frame of identity of people with housing challenges is further reinforced and perhaps perpetuated by the services pledging to assist them. This process of othering gives acceptance

---

[6] *Ibid.*

to the use of social control methods to compel individuals into compliance, without considering the other reasons why one may face housing challenges.

Thus, an expansion from the conventional individualised case-based conversation to a discussion of larger societal structures that sustain and drive injustices towards people facing housing challenges is a necessity, if we want to address homelessness holistically. This then puts the social worker in a unique position and requires a critical examination of our role. Are we also part of the system that contributes to the continued oppression of people with housing challenges? How we may choose to intervene or not will have implications for the well-being and liberation of those whom we are bound by our mission to enhance.

This gives rise to questions on how one addresses these systematic challenges that go beyond casework practice? Additionally, how do we continue working with systems that consistently disregard the identities of those whom we work for, while concurrently seeking to advance the hopes and wishes, and respecting their individual dignity? When faced with such challenges, it is easy to adhere into the flow of the environment around us or ground ourselves further in professional knowledge and models to look for options and other methods. Yet, in the process of doing so, do we continue to forsake the very people whom we have committed to empower?

Community Organising for Survival

The seemingly bleak outlook faced when engaging in issues surrounding homelessness from a FSC's perspective has compelled the continued reflection in our own social work practice and the experimentation of ideas. Within the multiple iterations of practice methods, a fundamental social work function of community development and organising came to the forefront. If we are interested in social change for the betterment of the human condition, the community context, group processes and community participation cannot be ignored.

In Vasoo's reflection on the state of community development in Singapore, community organisations are encouraged to create more opportunities for citizens to participate in decision-making about the problems they faced.[7] This frame allowed more interesting practice questions to emerge. What if we held our professional thoughts and asked those with housing challenges themselves, how they would like to be helped? What do they think about homelessness in Singapore? Do they even agree with the label "homeless" that is often so readily affixed to them? Is it possible to organise them into a collective for group action to advocate for themselves? Through the exploration of these questions, we began our community development journey from "homeless" to survivalists.

From Outreach to Organising

Outreach at ECP was already an existing practice for several years among the social workers at the FSC. The motivation to begin the outreach in 2011 was to engage and understand those who were living at ECP, especially since there were many who did not approach the FSC for assistance. The intensity varied depending on the context of both the agency and the environment. In the beginning phases, outreach was done weekly for continuity in engagement to introduce ourselves and build trust. There were also seasonal periods where the number of people living at ECP would increase and require more engagement. Additionally, occasional community events such as BBQs were organised as part of the rapport-building process. When the position of the social worker and knowledge of services available became more certain to the community, the outreach intensity reduced to monthly rather than weekly.

An outcome that is frequently hoped for in doing outreach is to connect people to services, which was a primary objective during the early iterations of practice. Through the relationships that were built, there were efforts to tap on the assets and strengths of some of the community members living at ECP, for example, informing new entrants about the available services, keeping an eye out for families with young children and distribution of resources.

While this asset and strengths-based perspective was helpful in creating a difference in our engagement, the tasks involved seemed to

---

[7] S Vasoo, "Community development in Singapore: New directions and challenges", *Asian Journal of Political Science*, 9(1), 2001, pp. 4–17.

supplement the functions of the agency rather than fulfilling the community's needs. Though there was some confluence between both interests at times, on hindsight, the slant towards the agency's functions were probably the result of the social workers' positioning and the fact that social workers were driving the agenda setting, goals and tasks. Participation in these tasks was also limited to a minority of interested individuals as most were passive about getting involved.

Thus, community organising methods sought to further evolve these efforts to be more collaborative and balanced, and at the same time creating platforms for the community to engage, collectivise and participate in tasks that they were interested in. Instead of being directive and coming in with a position of the expert, we shifted our focus towards the coordination of people and resources, as well as facilitating group decision-making. The subsequent sections outline the collectivising process involved in moving from an individual case perspective to a community of survivalists.

Processes in Organising

Building relationships to collectivise

As discussed, outreach was already an ongoing activity among the social workers. However, the intentions of outreach further evolved beyond connecting people to services. It became a method to build relationships with people regardless of whether they were existing clients or not, or whether they were interested in services or not. It was a process of engaging individuals with a genuine interest in their well-being, life stories, strengths and needs. It is through the understanding of the personhood of the individual that we can then recognise and acknowledge their own identity.

During the engagement, should one require and consent to individualised case-based services, a social worker would be assigned for further follow-up. Engagement with the service user during the outreach practice will continue even though they were already receiving case management services by a different social worker. Tapping on these individual relationships that were already formed, we then shifted to group-based conversations by inviting them for community meetings. Meanwhile, individualised outreach was still done with new entrants who may not be as familiar with group-based engagements until they were ready to join the collective.

Many who were staying at ECP were already familiar with one another, but did not meet to discuss common issues they faced as a community. While there were conversations between some individuals, there were no existing platforms for larger discussions. Hence, the community meetings, open to all who were living at ECP, became a place where they could discuss tensions they face and act upon them together. The outreach modality of engaging individuals for conversations thus evolved into having group engagements through monthly community meetings, held at a specified time and place at ECP.

Outreach plays an important function in community development and was the foundation of the engagement with the ECP community. While outreach can be viewed as a task to promote services, having a wider goal to build relationships with people enabled the conversation to move beyond service provision and individualisation. The community meetings that evolved then kickstarted the process of collectivising. Without a strong rapport between the social workers and the individuals in the community, the community meetings and collectivising may not have taken off.

Collective identity

Cohen extensively discusses how communities are symbolically constructed through a system of values and norms that give rise to a sense of meaning and identity to its members.[8] Similarly, in the study of social movements, McAdam raises the importance of having a shared meaning about a situation, which provides a common identifiable frame to help drive and sustain the movement.[9] This collective action frame should be based on meanings that community members can emotionally connect and identify with, which anchors the group and keeps them continually

---

[8] Anthony P. Cohen, *The Symbolic Construction of Community* (Chichester: Ellis Horwood, 1985).
[9] Doug McAdam, *Political Process and the Development of Black Insurgency, 1930–1970*, 2nd edn. (Chicago, IL: University of Chicago Press, 1999).

interested and actively engaged.[10] Thus, a powerful frame can become the glue that binds the collective and a springboard for collective action. However, such cultural factors are often underemphasised in social movements despite their indispensable nature.[11]

To collectively explore these themes about identities and meaning with the community at ECP, we tapped on the community meetings and started to ask the practice questions raised earlier on how they viewed themselves as well as homelessness as an issue. The explorations were done at ECP in a more intensive weekly group work setting to collectively raise their consciousness as a group.

"Homeless" to survivalists

In the discussions about the perceptions of homelessness, the residents at ECP were fully aware of the common perceptions about them in public discourse. They were conscious of the negative labels often affixed on them without choice and did not identify with the socially constructed norms around homelessness. To them, the image of a "homeless" person would be one who sleeps on cardboards in the open, has poor hygiene, has no cash for food and is dependent on the welfare system for sustenance. They also disagreed with the ascribed values of being lazy and unmotivated.

The dissatisfaction with the labels pinned on them were also stirred up by the impacts of having these labels. They recounted stories about their interactions with formal agencies, where these messages were reinforced on to them. When they do not act in accordance to the agencies' recommendations, they are then blamed for creating the challenges they faced, deemed as non-genuine cases and may have enforcement action taken against them.

---

[10] Toorjo Ghose, "Politicizing political society: Mobilization among sex workers in Songachi, India", in Ania Loomba and Ritty A. Lukose (eds.), *South Asian Feminisms* (Durham, NC: Duke University Press, 2012), pp. 285–305.
[11] Doug McAdam, *Political Process and the Development of Black Insurgency, 1930–1970*.

During the explorations with the community about their identities, they preferred to be known as survivalists rather than as "homeless" people. It was a word generated by the community themselves and was a frame they identified greatly with. They saw themselves as owning their own shelter that they have, being able to work to support themselves and not being abusive of the welfare system. All members of the community at that time were not receiving financial aid from any formal agencies. Despite facing their own challenges that include housing, they still possess the strength, the desire and determination to survive these difficulties and persevere on even though they may get overwhelming.

This identity frame thus challenges the current narrative about people facing housing challenges. Rather than creating categories of haves and have-nots between the homed and "homeless", ascribing labels and values in these categories and finding "expert" solutions to these categories of needs, the survivalist frame attempts to eliminate this binary thinking. It expresses that we all have our own challenges to face and overcome, whether the challenge is housing related or not, and the belief that everyone has their own inner strengths to cope and problem-solve in this journey for survival and personal betterment.

Organising around the identity

The process of collectively exploring this theme with the survivalists facilitated a large degree of affiliation with the survivalist identity frame. The validation of their personhood and their experiences at ECP further influenced the strong emotional connection to the frame, providing further glue to the organising effort and solidarity among the community members. This further shifted the position where members continue to participate in community meetings not just from the relationships built with the social workers but also for each other.

A second stage in the organisation's effort was the rallying behind the survivalist identity frame for collective action. The strong identification naturally led to an active interest in how to raise this identity to the relevant systems and the public to counter the existing narratives. During a dialogue at a community meeting about the community's decision on appearing in public media interviews, this collective identity seemingly helped spur the group to decide to take risks together. Prior to the collectivising process, appearing in any media or in public view tended to be a contentious issue for the survivalists. They tended to experience negative impacts from any public attention and became wary whenever there was any media or external scrutiny. However, with the knowledge that their alternative collective identity could challenge the existing dominant discourses on homelessness, they became willing to take on the risks of media interviews and consented to furthering their identity in public spaces.

Thus, the importance of having a framework to organise around cannot be underemphasised. The collaborative process of constructing identity with the survivalists helped to build solidarity within the group as well as to invite them to take action for themselves.

Critical consciousness

The concept of *conscientizacao* or critical consciousness, introduced by Freire, refers to the learning of how to perceive the social, political and economic contradictions in one's reality, in order to take action against the oppressive elements of that reality.[12] Developing critical consciousness was a key mechanism proposed by Freire in the pursuit of human liberation and the process of becoming more human and was a foundational guiding concept in our survivalist journey.[13]

Building up awareness

The journey started with establishing the extent of both the social workers' and survivalists' understanding of their current reality through group dialogues. While there was already some cognizance among both groups about their current perceived realities, there seemed to be some maladaptation to them.

---

[12] Paulo Freire, *Pedagogy of the Oppressed: 30th Anniversary Edition* (New York, NY: Continuum, 2000).
[13] *Ibid.*

For a social worker, one might get disillusioned about one's role and position, especially when having to manage cases with housing challenges that are particularly demanding and with seemingly little options. Without guidance, one may react with pessimism and negativity towards the work. Hence, the openness to discuss these challenges and uncertainties in a group setting was a starting point for the team. The group context allowed for alternative viewpoints to emerge, as a base to discuss potential adjustments to the team's practices, and the assurance that realities are not fixed but are transformable.

On the contrary, the survivalists tend to also have a great awareness of their challenging reality, as most would have already tried all means that they knew of to secure housing. They may become upset about their limited choices and either project their anger onto others in unhealthy ways or even disengage from help or other relationships. Similarly, the group setting allowed for learning from others' experiences, hearing from different social workers and, most importantly, the belief in the ability to effect change as a community.

While individuals may have varying understandings based on their own worldviews, the group-based facilitation provides alternative challenges to one's own perspectives to continue building new realities. This base level of awareness would then help to inform the organising processes and topics to discuss among the social workers and survivalists.

Action and reflection

Freire proposes for the praxis of action and reflection through dialogues as a means of liberation.[14] It is the process through which learners develop an understanding of the world so that they can transform it. Action without reflection is empty action, while reflection without action is verbalism.[15] Both are equally important in the collectivising process for the practitioners and survivalists alike and are done simultaneously.

As practitioners, it was important for our engagement with the survivalists to take a backseat at times, to critically reflect on our work.

---

[14] *Ibid.*
[15] *Ibid.*

While there was ongoing community organising, there were also times of reflection about our position, direction, dilemmas and tensions, as well as our own ruminations arising from dialoguing with the survivalists. The dialogues among the team then further shaped the organising process with the survivalists.

Among the survivalists, reflection involved group processing about the circumstances they are in, to raise consciousness collectively. They were also involved in planning for how they envision the changes to look like, followed by acting upon the world. For example, following the process of negotiating identity and how they would like to be identified as survivalists, there was an "open house" event planned together with the survivalists. Other social service professionals were invited to the event, where the survivalists presented their stories and identity through tours, actions and conversations. Through the dialogue, a space was created for mutual influence and transformation in the understanding of homelessness and each other's self-perceptions.

Upon completion of the interaction there was also the space to again engage in reflection, where we processed with the group about their experiences and learning. The tasks required in the collective process thus mainly revolved around concurrent action and reflection activities, while continuing to strengthen identity and build relationships with the survivalists.

Integrative Social Work Practice

The approaches used were borne out of the context of social work practice within a FSC attempting to engage in the complex social issue of homelessness. While this chapter focuses on the community organising effort, ongoing individualised case management and other practice methods were still done with those who opted for services to allow for more in-depth work. Thus, the entire intervention endeavour would also include the other complementary work done alongside the organising effort, in an integrated manner.

Social events were commonly held as a place for action, where the survivalist can participate in planning and implementation. These were necessary to further build solidarity through fun and shared experiences.

Apart from the direct work functions, there is continued networking with various stakeholders, as well as research efforts done by the social workers. At the current stage, these indirect functions of the work are mainly fulfilled by the social workers rather than with the survivalists. This remains a current limitation, though there are thoughts on how to further involve the survivalists themselves in the networking process and research projects in the future.

Challenges

High Mobility of Survivalists

One of the challenges in sustaining the community organising effort is the high mobility among the survivalists. Homelessness can be transient in nature, and there will be continuous entrants into the community as well as exits from the geographical community at ECP. This can make solidarity building challenging.

For new entrants, discovering such an ecosystem can be helpful to get some support, but can be equally intimidating due to the trust required to open up to others whom they have never met before. Because of past life experiences and fears of involvement in illicit or anti-social behaviours, some may choose to not get involved. Others may also not connect emotionally to the survivalist identity and may not derive deeper meaning in the collectivising processes. For others who were once part of the community and had exited, they may also not want to return and continue to be engaged. Homelessness is a traumatic experience to some, and they may not want to be reminded of their past histories or tensions.

With the community membership constantly in flux, it is imperative for the community organisers to remain inclusive, mobilise members to help one another and continue to remind members of the objectives and collective identity of the group, to sustain the group. This requires continual effort from the organisers, leaving much of the responsibilities of sustaining the collectivising effort still with the organisers at this juncture. Thus, though attempts to redistribute power towards the community were made, it is still imbalanced, until stable leadership is built among the community members.

"Client" Mindset

Another challenge among some survivalists is this sense of dependency and disempowerment in making decisions. This may come from their past family experiences or previous engagements with social services and other public agencies, where they were often provided options, education, advice or even assistance, without a consultative and collaborative discussion. Thus, they might expect the social worker to come up with solutions for their challenges or provide for their needs, rather than having discussions to work together on what works best for them.

New entrants commonly present with such expectations, and it takes continued participation in the various platforms created to be able to shift one's mindset from a client passively receiving services to a person having the space to influence how he or she would like to be helped and actively doing it for himself or herself. This also requires discipline from the community organisers to be less prescriptive and be mindful of the process of encouraging participation and listening to the voice of others.

Organisational Systems

Currently, the way social service agencies in Singapore are structured can be a challenge for social workers to engage in such community development practices. Services in Singapore heavily lean on the social planning approach according to Rothman's conceptual model of community practice.[16] Programmes and services are often put in place to fulfil community needs, and to ensure accountability or to measure outcomes, tasks or outcome indicators are often used.[17] However, in the process of developing these indicators, most communities are often not consulted. When communities propose alternative tasks or approaches, a social worker is then in a difficult position on having to balance between both agendas. As an employee of the agency, how would one get evaluated based on the pre-identified tasks or activities that may not be carried out? Would there be sufficient variance allowed within an agency's environment to

---

[16] Jack Rothman, "The interweaving of community intervention approaches", *Journal of Community Practice*, 3(3–4), 1996, pp. 69–99.
[17] *Ibid.*

allow communities to direct the organising effort, without impacting an employee's position?

This inherent dilemma in balancing organisational goals and community goals will be commonly faced by social workers in community practice. Organisations and social workers who would like to use community work approaches should be aware of such potential conflicts and be mindful of the perspectives of various groups as well as their own values and beliefs. Ultimately, one would need to constantly reflect about practice and one's position and be mindful of whom we are accountable to as a social worker.

Future Work

Involving "Clients" in Intervention in Cultural Action

Community work in social services is often framed in terms of programmes, services and tasks that are available to clients in the various communities. This is a valid perspective of community development, as it contributes to the development of resources available to people. However, client participation in decision-making may not be encouraged in such models. The word "client" itself invokes the notion of one who is a recipient of services, a customer or a beneficiary. By framing one's identity as a passive recipient, it demarcates spaces where one can be involved or not.

Thus, how we view community work in Singapore should not be limited to programmes or activities done for client groups but done together with these groups. Citizenship participation among the have-nots has to include themes of redistribution of power and having the ability to affect the outcome of the process, rather than tokenism or even non-participation.[18] Community work practice should create space and platforms for degrees of citizen power, which would be the responsibility of practitioners to include. Additionally, as part of the mission of social work, there must be unequivocal interest in communities who are vulnerable and oppressed.

---

[18] Sherry R. Arnstein, "A ladder of citizen participation", *Journal of the American Institute of Planners*, 4(35), 1969, pp. 216–224.

Participation and power should also not be limited to tangible tasks and programmes but also cultural identity. Being owners of one's self and framing of identity is as equally important. The degree of participation is often influenced by how identities are constructed that gives power to some over others. Challenging binary and exclusionary terms should be part of community practice to empower people with how they would like themselves to be recognised and identified. This necessitates practitioners to engage in individual stories and not be patronising about life histories and identities.

Community Development Work with Other Oppressed Groups

The work discussed here is not limited to the context of people with housing challenges alone but is applicable to other groups facing discrimination and social exclusion. There are certainly many communities in Singapore that this approach might be applicable for.

The model discussed here was within a context of a social service agency with unique functions and responsibilities. Other groups that are interested in such work would need to evaluate their own resources and be mindful of how they would like to frame their community work intervention. Constant critical reflection and seeking clarity on one's role and responsibilities in the context of the larger macroenvironment would further serve as a guide for social workers interested in social change.

Chapter 11

The Future of Community Development: Issues and Challenges

S Vasoo

Some pertinent questions should be raised about the future of community development[1] and the challenges ahead[2]. What is the optimistic or at worst the pessimistic picture facing community development? These are not necessarily binary questions. The responses are not a black or white as community issues are dynamic and changing. Let us examine the pessimistic side first and then the optimistic aspects.

Pessimistic Community Scenario

The downside will be that communities will be so self-centric and socially divisive that individuals and community groups are at loggerhead over

---

[1] In this article, community development is defined as efforts either jointly or on their own of Government, corporate sector community organisations, not for profit groups and or voluntary welfare organisations (VWOs) to promote community betterment and community problem-solving by involving people based on mutual help or self-help and planned changes. The outcome is community ownership in promoting community well-being.
[2] Stephen Hawking, *Can We Predict the Future in Brief — Answers to Questions* (UK: John Murray Publishers, 2018), pp. 87–98.

socio-political and resources allocation matters. Conflicts amongst community groups over all social and livelihood matters can become so protracted and eventually be untenable for people to co-operate and work for the interest of the majority living in the community. If the community has to slide down to this state of affair, then people will become more individualistic and less open to extend mutual care and support in community problem-solving. At worst, the neighbourhoods will be hollowed out by the better endowed leaving first then others, to more vibrant and supportive communities. The possibility of a pessimistic scene can carry some negative consequences. This situation can provoke some groups to surface to find some workable solutions in the midst of contending forces in the community, which try to oppress change for community betterment.[3] However, the community efforts will indeed be very trying to improve and put things right.

Optimistic Community Scenario

With an optimistic picture, the community setting will be lively and vibrant as people will look beyond themselves and see one another as a supportive network and willing to share and care for with all others better or less endowed. Those who are better and resourceful will be prepared to share their surpluses with those who are poorer. Altruistic behaviours are likely to be displayed by people and this is indicative that they have social and community responsibility. Community development efforts must help promote such altruistic behaviours as this will encourage the growth and development of more social support networks and consequently act as precursors for the formation of social and community agencies and even social enterprises. In communities with optimism, people normally aspire to be progressive and innovative to find creative ways in community problem-solving. It is envisaged that there will be many types of resources in the community and these can be tapped to support those in need of them. Hence, a social exchange bank with the depository of both human needs and supply services can be established to promote social

---

[3] David Chan (ed.), *Public Trust in Singapore* (Singapore: World Scientific Publishing, 2018), pp. 3–18.

exchanges at affordable cost to users. In fact, with the development of artificial intelligence based on aggregative technologies, a number of community-based social exchange banks can be formed. Good corporate governance will be required to help such social exchange banks to function effectively and in the interest of the community.[4]

Community development can be efficacious if it enhances the development of social and human capital by enabling social and community groups to develop self-help and mutual aid co-operatives. These social set-ups or enterprises can address social issues such as problems of loneliness, need for care and support, requirements for educational enrichments, acquiring and upgrading vocational skills, delinquency, crime and security issues, childcare and healthcare needs, unemployment and employability matters, and personal and family related difficulties. Notably, some of these social issues are tackled by social and community agencies in their own agency-centric ways. It will be more effective and efficient to pay more attention on the development of better inter-community agency partnership and efforts.[5]

Against this backdrop, it will be appropriate to examine the community development efforts in Singapore. In the last four decades or so, it has focused much on social and recreational activities. Consequently, community organisations or groups have gravitated to become task or programme-centred. The outsourcing of community services to the private sector is becoming a norm and this can affect the quality of services contracted out.

Some Issues

First, the increasing moves on outsourcing community activities and services can make community organisations insular and they then become task- or activity-centred and slowly digress from being people-centred which is aimed in promoting self-help and community ownership.

---

[4] Ibid., pp. 61–68.
[5] S Vasoo, "Investment for the Social Sector to Tackle Key Social Issues in Critical Issues", in S Vasoo and Bilveer Singh (eds.), *Critical Issues in Asset Building in Singapore's Development* (Singapore: World Scientific Publishing, 2018), pp. 21–36.

Hence, many community organisations and groups have adopted a less outreaching approach to understand the changing needs of the community. In the longer term such a move will make them more detached from keeping in touch with the needs of people who are uninvolved or at the margins.

Second, the leadership of community organisations is graying. More attention should be devoted to enlist resourceful younger residents to help manage them. Many community organisations have become gerentocratic and can be less responsive to the changing needs of the neighbourhoods. Consequently, they can become senior citizen clubs, which will only meet the needs of one specific group of the resident population, namely the elderly. So far, punctuated attempts have been made to renew the leadership and as such, it is unlikely to rejuvenate community organisations.

Third, it is observed that the rate of participation of lower-income households and minorities is not as significant and this could be due to the less tangible benefits offered by the programmes delivered by community groups and organisations. The participation of both minorities and lower-income families is critical in maintaining social cohesion and community bonding. Hence, more concrete services are to be provided to meet their social and economic needs. This will address the public goods dilemma, as this will reduce their cost for participation. When community organisations do not bear in mind of this matter in their service delivery, both minorities and low-income households will not be motivated to participate in some mainstream community activities.

Fourth, another significant development in the older neighbourhoods of Singapore is the hollowing out of the more resourceful and younger residents. When this process accelerates, these neighbourhoods become eventually silver communities. A higher outflow of young people who are attracted by exuberant facilities of other New Towns also compounds this. It is anticipated that there will be a depletion of community and leadership resources in these neighbourhoods. This will inevitably slow down and become less attractive to new residents. Inevitability, social burdens for care will increase unless more community care services and support networks are encouraged through community development efforts.

Meeting the Challenges

Some challenges confronting community development in Singapore have been identified. It is therefore appropriate to discuss a few ideas to deal with these challenges. Policy makers, community leaders and social workers may consider undertaking to enhance community development efforts in the context of Singapore.

Enhancing Self-Help and Community Ownership

There should be less outsourcing contracts and more in-sourcing activities by mobilising residents to form not for profit organisations or social enterprises. Such attempts will provide more opportunities for residents to participate in decision making so that they can take ownership. More community care groups and support networks can be established. This will make participants not passive recipients of services and be engaged in problem solving. Community organisations widen the base of participation by residents forming various interest groups or task forces to work on various social issues and projects such as security watch and crime prevention, co-operative care services, improvements to recreational facilities, pollution control, thrift through micro-credit groups, and environmental enhancement projects. It will be useful to encourage residents to take charge in finding more effective ways to deal with local matters. In this case, the support of the Town Councils (TCs) and Community Development Councils (CDCs) will be helpful. This is truly be promoting community development as local residents will learn and find more realistic solutions to solve their specific needs and problems and become accountable for their decisions.

However, with the move towards information technology, more people could become impersonal, homebound, social interactions could be reduced, and social bonding could be threatened. Therefore, personalised outreaching efforts can be carried out with on-line contacts.

Leadership Rejuvenation and Organisational Renewal

It is observed that a significant number of grassroots leaders of community organisations in the mature housing estates are above 50 years old. These organisations face difficulties in recruiting younger residents to take up leadership.[6] With the graying of the organisational leadership, there is urgency to rejuvenate the leadership of community organisations by attracting younger professionals to participate them. It is not just sufficient to recruit them. Some committed older leaders must mentor them. With attachment to specific mentors, they can be better affiliated to the organisations and this will reduce attrition facing younger persons taking up leadership in organisations dominated by seniors. A rejuvenated leadership will continue to be vibrant and relevant to meet the needs and aspirations of younger generation of residents. We must also attract younger people-centred individuals to become community leaders and be given all the support to carry out community problem-solving activities. People-centred community leaders are usually proactive. They should not be piled up with so many tasks as this can make them suffer from burnout. More importantly, young leaders should be given management skills training so that they can understand the needs of residents. This can help make community organisations responsive to tackling emerging social needs.[7]

Reaching out to Lower Income Residents and Minorities

Singapore is an open economy and becoming more globalised. It is inevitable the residents with low skills are likely to be faced by depressed wages and this can lead to widening income gap.[8] Singaporeans with better skills are likely to move ahead while those with low skills and less literate in information technology will fall behind in income. Social stratification based on social-economic classes confounded by ethnicity may surface if excessive free market competition is not tempered. Consequently, social conflicts could emerge when political and racial fanatics emerge to

---

[6] S Vasoo, *Neighborhood Leaders Participation in Community Development* (Singapore: Academic Press, 1994); S Vasoo (2002), *New Directions in Community Development in Extending Frontiers* (Singapore: Eastern University Press, 2002), pp. 20–36.
[7] S Vasoo, "Community Development in Singapore; Issues and Challenges", in S Vasoo and Bilveer Singh (eds.), *Community Development Arenas in Singapore* (Singapore: World Scientific Publishing, 2019).
[8] Goh Chok Tong, *Prime Minister's National Day Rally Speech 2000* (Singapore Government: Ministry of Information and the Arts), pp. 22–25.

capitalise the situation. Our community harmony and cohesion could be fractured.[9] As such, community organisations, namely CDCs together with other NGOs can take preventive measures to deliver community-based self-help programmes such as social and educational assistance, computer training, educational head start for children of low-income families, child care services, youth vocational guidance and counseling programmes, family-life and development activities, and continuing learning programmes to help the socially disadvantaged groups. As a long-term measure for people capability building, it is important for us to develop more educational head start projects for low-income children in the nursery age group. The increase of such projects through community partnership of various self-help groups, unions, co-operatives and not for profit organizations will help children from disadvantaged background to level up to acquire productive skills for their future livelihood. Matched savings schemes tied up with such projects can be initiated. These community development efforts can help to reduce the social frictions between classes and ethnic groups. Fanatics and extremists will find it less tempting to exploit the race card as the problems facing low-income families cut across all ethnic groups. Therefore, the realistic solution is to help level up the capabilities of all disadvantaged children despite their color or ethnicity.[10]

Singapore is indeed a multi-racial society comprising of Chinese (74.3%), Malays (13.4%), Indians (9%) and others (3.2%).[11] It is crucial that various efforts both at the social policy and community activities levels are consciously implemented to generate better racial understanding. Where necessary steps are to be taken to encourage multi-racial involvement of residents and community leaders.[12] To strengthen Singapore's

---

[9] Lee Kuan Yew, *From Third World to First — The Singapore Story 1965–2000* (Singapore: Times Media, 2000), pp. 143–157.

[10] S Vasoo, "Investment for the Social Sector to Tackle Key Social Issues", in S Vasoo and Bilveer Singh (eds.), *Critical Issues in Asset Building in Singapore's Development* (Singapore: World Scientific Publishing, 2018), pp. 21–36.

[11] *Statistics on Demographic Characteristics*, (Singapore: Department of Statistics, 2018).

[12] Raj Vasil (2000), *Governing Singapore* (Leonards NSW: Allen and Unwin, 2000), pp. 84–85; S Vasoo and Bilveer Singh, "Introduction", in S Vasoo and Bilveer Singh (eds.), *Critical Issues in Asset Building in Singapore's Development* (Singapore: World Scientific Publishing, 2018).

social landscape, it is desirable to encourage multi-ethnic participation in social and recreation activities organised by grassroots organisations, civic and social organisations, TCs and CDCs. In the longer term, social harmony is critical to the social and economic well-being of Singapore's communities of different ethnic persuasions.

Renewal and Rejuvenation of Ageing Neighbourhoods

It will be evident that in the next two decades or so, we will see a number of 'silver' neighbourhoods emerging. If attempts by public housing authorities to renew and rejuvenate these neighbourhoods are slower than population aging in these places, then they will become listless and socially run down. Local social and economic activities will slow down and younger people will not be attracted to live in these neighbourhoods as seniors will dominate the localities. Ultimately, there will be more families facing the need for care of elderly parents or relatives.[13] As many of these families have working family members, they will face the burden of care. Social breakdowns are likely without accessible social support and community care services delivered at the local level. Therefore, there will be demands for more community-based programmes to cater to the needs of families who have frail aged family members. The number of such families is expected to increase in the next decade. In light of this situation, more community groups, voluntary welfare organisations together with the involvement of residents as well the hospitals, will have to work as partners to provide community care services such as home-help, meals service, daycare, integrated housing and community nursing. Here, community care co-operatives could be formed to offer services, which will be more convenient and accessible to the families with frail elderly needing care and attention. There is potential for this type of social enterprise to be established with participation of families as one of the stakeholders.[14]

---

[13] *Report by Inter-Ministerial Committee on Ageing* (Singapore: Ministry of Community Development, 1999).

[14] S Vasoo and Kalyani Mehata Mehta, "Organization and Delivery of Long-Term Care in Singapore: Present Issues and Future Challenges", *Journal of Aging & Social Policy*, 13(2/3), 2001, pp. 185–201.

Conclusion

Community development efforts must encourage people to take ownership of the various social and economic activities, which are delivered, in the various neighbourhoods in partnership with a number of groups. To have impact, community organisations or groups cannot continue to assume that they know what residents want but to outreach to appraise their social needs or requirements. In short, community development should promote self-help and the focus should be to encourage mutual help and not dependency and helplessness.

As Singapore becomes more globalised, social needs and problems will become more challenging to solve, as it will require the efforts of a number of key players. Therefore, community problem-solving will require the partnership of several parties. The partnership model of the Government, community organisations and groups, corporate sector and philanthropic individuals can be encouraged as such a model, emphasis on the belief in sharing the social burdens. All partners involved in community problem-solving have shared social responsibilities. Both manpower and matching grants are allocated to various projects to be carried out by community groups, social enterprises, non-profit sector and community organisations.

As community needs become more complex and challenging there will be an increase in interest groups which will lobby resource and policyholders to advance their group's agenda. Therefore, leaders of community organisations and community groups will have to be more objective and work for the interest of the majority. To have viable and effective community organisations, there must be active attempts to recruit, motivate and retain younger leaders to commit to find ways to meet the interest of the wider good. Unless we have such committed community leaders, it will be more trying to fortify the social health of the community.

Community development must include amongst its strategies that social and community workers are to be trained and equipped with social and analytical skills so that they can visualise clearly the current and emerging trends in social issues and problems facing various neighbourhood communities in Singapore. The use of aggregative technologies to pool resources both within and outside the communities to set up a social exchange bank could be implemented for community so that there could be more effective responses to problem solving. As most communities have many types of their own resources in such areas like social, vocational, educational, medical, healthcare, technological, engineering financial, environmental, agricultural and aqua-culture, could be pooled and deployed to those groups that need them. All in all, community development must play a more prominent role in helping individuals and community groups to level up so that social gaps can be narrowed and reduced.[15] This can reduce or prevent serious social conflicts and help to inoculate against social infections in our communities.

---

[15] David Chan, *People Matter* (Singapore: World Scientific Publishing, 2015), pp. 49–54; S Vasoo, "Investment for the Social Sector to Tackle Key Social Issues", in S Vasoo and Bilveer Singh (eds), *Critical Issues in Asset Building in Singapore's Development* (Singapore: World Scientific Publishing, 2018), pp. 21–36.